ON THE
TECHNIQUE
OF ACTING

ON THE
TECHNIQUE
OF ACTING

BY MICHAEL CHEKHOV

Edited and with an Introduction by Mel Gordon

Preface and Afterword by Mala Powers

HarperPerennial
A Division of HarperCollinsPublishers

HarperCollins books may be purchased for educational, business, or sales
promotional use. For information please write: Special Markets Department,
HarperCollins Publishers, Inc., 10 East 53rd Street,
New York, NY 10022.

Designed by Ruth Kolbert

The Library of Congress has catalogued the earlier edition of this book as follows:

Chekhov, Michael, 1891–1955.
On the technique of acting / Michael Chekhov; edited by Mel
Gordon; preface and afterword by Mala Powers.
   p.   m.
Rev. ed. of: To the actor. 1st Barnes & Noble Books ed. 1985.
Includes index.
ISBN 0-06-055267-0 / ISBN 0-06-096524-X (pbk.)
1. Acting. I. Chekhov, Michael, 1891–1955. To the actor.
II. Gordon, Mel. III. Title.
PN2061.C538   1991   90-55493
792'.028—dc20

ISBN 0-06-273037-1 (pbk.)
   00 01 RRD-H 20 19 18 17 16 15 14

CONTENTS

Drawings 1–7 follow page 68.
Illustrations follow page 118.

ACKNOWLEDGMENTS

The writings of Michael Chekhov and his acting technique survive today only because of the extraordinary efforts, sacrifice, and devotion of his supporters and students. We especially wish to express thanks:

To Beatrice Straight, who along with Dorothy and Leonard Elmhurst provided a haven of ideal creative conditions at Dartington Hall in England and later at Ridgefield, Connecticut, in which Michael Chekhov could freely experiment, teach, direct, and refine his ideas and then communicate and write down his technique of acting so that it can be passed on to future generations of actors—

To Deirdre Hurst du Prey, not only for her invaluable assistance to Chekhov in preparing the original manuscript of this book but also for her many years of faithfulness and dedication in the work of recording and transcribing Chekhov's ideas and words—

To Dr. Georgette Boner, whose support, encouragement, understanding, and keen mind helped Chekhov greatly in his early process of identifying and formulating a training technique for actors—

To George Shdanoff, who shared with Chekhov the work, excitement, and joy of the Chekhov Theatre and who, as both teacher and director, contributed to and participated in many pedagogic experiments with the principles presented in this book—

To Hurd Hatfield and Paul Marshall Allen for their expertise and literary contribution to the formative version of Chekhov's manuscript—

And to the late Xenia Chekhov, who contributed so much to this book and to the life of Michael Chekhov through her very special qualities of patience, understanding, and love.

Mel Gordon
Mala Powers

Michael Chekhov was one of the most extraordinary actors and teachers of the twentieth century. From his professional debut at the Moscow Art Theatre's experimental First Studio in 1913 until his death in Hollywood forty-two years later, Chekhov electrified Russian-, French-, German-, and English-speaking audiences, who often waited in feverish anticipation at his dressing room doors and backstage exits. In the early part of his career, critics, who had never seen such a seamless and startling mix of deeply emoted realism within a portrayal of grotesque fantasy, even questioned whether what Chekhov did on the stage was actually "acting." It was as if the real characters from the pages of Shakespeare, Gogol, Dickens, Dostoyevsky, and Strindberg had mysteriously dropped down to earth, momentarily interacting with other performers, who then appeared wooden and stagebound.

Michael Chekhov also had the unusual capacity to enthuse and excite some of Europe's and America's greatest stage and film practitioners, from celebrated directors like Yevgeny Vakhtangov and Max Reinhardt to established Broadway and Hollywood actors like Stella Adler and Gregory Peck. Marilyn Monroe once called Chekhov the most powerful spiritual influence in her life—after Abraham Lincoln. Yul Brynner confessed that Chekhov opened all the doors of theatrical art for him at the very beginning of his studies. And during the twenties and thirties, Konstantin Stanislavsky (1863–1938) frequently referred to Chekhov, a radical challenger to Stanislavsky's own System of modern acting, as "his most brilliant student."

Like so many of Russia's artists who came of age in the twenties, Chekhov's life underwent scores of transformations and reversals. A nephew of the playwright and short story writer Anton Chekhov, he battled charges of nepotism in the theatre and chronic alcoholism, which he inherited from his father, a philosopher and inventor manqué. Born in St. Petersburg on August 16, 1891, Michael (christened Mikhail Aleksandrovich) exhibited a wild and passionate temperament throughout his childhood. Encouraged by a peasant nanny, young Chekhov engaged in a variety of theatre games and character impersonations. In a 1944 autobiographical account, Chekhov remembered that period clearly: "I took the first piece of clothing I came across, put it on and felt: *who I am*. The improvisations were serious or comic, depending on the costume. No matter what I did, Nanny's reaction was always the same: she rocked with her long, whistling laughter, which turned to tears."

In 1907, Chekhov entered the Alexei Suvorin Dramatic School, where he excelled in comic roles. After two years of

indifferent training, he played the title part in Alexei Tolstoy's *Czar Fyodor Ivanovich,* which was presented in a special
performance before Czar Nikolas II. Backstage, young Chekhov was asked by the awkward Czar how his false nose was
affixed to his face. Accidentally, Chekhov dirtied the Czar's
glove. That night, according to Chekhov, several performers
dreamed independently of assassinating Nikolas.

Three years later, the twenty-one-year-old Chekhov was
already an established character actor at the prestigious Maly
Theatre. Stanislavsky took a personal interest in the nephew
of Anton Chekhov and invited him to audition for the more
prestigious Moscow Art Theatre, which was then at the peak
of its international renown. Despite a nerve-racking recitation, Chekhov was accepted into the theatrical institution.

At the Moscow Art Theatre's innovative First Studio,
Chekhov fell under the direct tutelage of the Armenian genius, Yevgeny Vakhtangov. Their personal and professional
relationship, although close, was filled with complications
and rivalries that were often manifested in practical jokes,
some of which led to real violence. On tour in the spring of
1915, for example, the two roommates created a game, "the
trained ape," whereby they took turns each morning acting
the part of the "ape." The "ape" crawled out of bed remaining on all fours, and prepared the coffee. Until the breakfast
was fixed, the other had the right to beat the "ape." For
Chekhov, and maybe for Vakhtangov, too, the game had
deeper psychological implications. Finally, the ape-Chekhov
"mutinied," and an actual fight broke out, with Chekhov
losing a tooth and Vakhtangov almost suffering from asphyxi-
ation.

During the MAT's 1912–13 seasons, Chekhov had walk-
on parts in various productions, including the Gordon Craig
Hamlet. During one performance of Molière's *The Imaginary
Invalid,* Stanislavsky reprimanded young Chekhov for "having too much fun with the part" of one of the supernumerary
physicians. Chekhov was shocked by the master's admonish-

ment. Wasn't *The Imaginary Invalid* a comedy? Therefore, wasn't a certain element of fun called for? While professing perfect belief in Stanislavsky's System of modern acting, Chekhov found himself in trouble with its creator from the very start.

Cast by Richard Boleslavsky in the First Studio's test production of Dutch playwright Herman Heijermans's *The Wreck of the "Good Hope,"* in 1913, Chekhov created quite a stir. He took the minor role of Kobe, the idiot fisherman, and transformed him into a creature of pathos and intense lyricism, altering the character, through movement and makeup, from a low comic type into a sincere and morbid seeker of the truth. For the audience, Chekhov's minor role became a new focus in the play. When criticized that his notion of Kobe was not what the playwright intended, Chekhov replied that he went beyond the playwright and the play to find Kobe's true character.

The idea that an actor can "go beyond the playwright or the play" is the first key to understanding the Chekhov Technique and how it differed from Stanislavsky's early teachings. Chekhov claimed that the impulse "to go beyond" came to him during his earlier apprenticeship at the Maly Theatre. During a 1910 performance of Nikolai Gogol's *Inspector General,* Chekhov watched one of his teachers, Boris Glagolin, in the lead part of Khlestakov. Suddenly, a revelation, a "kind of mental shift," overtook Chekhov: "It became clear to me that Glagolin plays the part of Khlestakov *not like others,* although I had never seen anyone else in that part. And this feeling, 'not like others,' arose in me."

Over a period of time Chekhov's acting goals changed. The "conquest of the audience" at the Maly and the relaxed and realistic portraits of the Moscow Art Theatre gave way to a quest for extraordinary character interpretations. In a sense, Chekhov had turned Stanislavsky's acting training on its head. Instead of the System's two-part Work on Oneself followed by Work on One's Role, Chekhov made Imagination and Character Work his primary foundation. In the Chekhov Technique, every other kind of exercise would follow from them.

One apocryphal story may explain the theatrical and personal conflict between Stanislavsky and Chekhov. Asked by the teacher to enact a true-life dramatic situation as an exercise in Affective Memory, Chekhov recreated his wistful presence at his father's funeral. Overwhelmed by its fine detail and sense of truth, Stanislavsky embraced Chekhov, thinking that this was yet another proof of the power of real Affective Memory for the actor. Unfortunately, Stanislavsky later discovered that Chekhov's ailing father was, in fact, still alive. Chekhov's performance was based not on *recapturing* the experience but on a feverish *anticipation* of the event. Reprimanded once again, Chekhov was dropped from the class owing to "an overheated imagination."

With every First Studio production, Chekhov's imaginative creations found a growing number of fans. For Vakhtangov's *The Peace Festival* (1913), Chekhov prepared the role of Fribe, the family drunk, in his usual novel manner. Working against the standard portrayal of an alcoholic, Chekhov built the physical character on a madman's realization that each part of his body is dying in a separate and horrifying way. Chekhov believed that death on the stage should be shown as a slowing down and disappearance of time in the human psyche. He wanted the audience to feel this physical retardation and even see the point where the slowing tempo ceases altogether as the character vainly fights off death. It was a *coup de théâtre*.

The First Studio's adaptation of Charles Dickens's *The Cricket on the Hearth* in 1915 fully established Chekhov the performer. Cast as Caleb, the frightened but kindly toymaker, Chekhov insisted on personally inventing and building all the mechanical toys for the production. His character came to him slowly as he visualized an old man seated on a chair and began to imagine the character's every action.

Blending Dostoyevskian morbidity with an all-embracing Tolstoyan love for his blind daughter, Chekhov's Caleb proved equal to Vakhtangov's villainous and mechanical Tarelton. Stanislavsky singled out Chekhov's performance as "almost brilliant."

At the end of 1915, Vakhtangov directed a First Studio production of Henning Berger's *The Deluge*. Double-casting himself and Chekhov in the part of Frazer, the bankrupt American merchant, their rivalry continued. Much to Vakhtangov's displeasure, Chekhov saw Frazer as a confused but loving Jewish businessman, although the character's ethnic background was nowhere indicated in the play. Using his hands to slap at the air like an hysterical girl and stumbling with bent knees against the saloon furniture, Chekhov was criticized for his overly physical and grotesque interpretation. It was true that Chekhov developed his character around an unusual mental image: Frazer was a man who unconsciously wanted to break through the clothes and skin of his competitors in order to make the deepest human contact possible; he wanted to physically touch their hearts. Yet of the two interpretations, Chekhov's and Vakhtangov's, audiences clearly preferred Chekhov's creation. Vakhtangov soon began to imitate Chekhov's Frazer as did other First Studio actors who later played the part. The number of Chekhov's Russian fans grew to several thousand.

Between 1913 and 1923 Chekhov appeared in twelve Moscow Art Theatre and independent productions, usually as a lead or in important supporting roles. His reputation as an actor and independent thinker increased dramatically during this period. But bouts of depression brought on by alcoholism, family deaths, war fever, revolution, and civil war often undermined his mental equilibrium and ability to act. Even so, the first two years after the Bolshevik victory (1918 and 1919) were especially crucial to Chekhov's spiritual and artistic breakthroughs.

During the run of the First Studio's *Twelfth Night*, Chekhov was reduced to a "gaunt brooding soul, weighed down by Russia's sorrows," according to Oliver Sayler, a visiting American critic. Played in his characteristic style of sharply etched contrasts, Chekhov's Malvolio was very much a crowd pleaser. In Chekhov's opening night performance, Shakespeare's sweet lyrical sensibilities became enmeshed in Malvolio's "swamp" of horrifying eroticism. But within a few weeks of the *Twelfth Night* premiere, Chekhov developed acute paranoia, believing that he both could "hear" and "see" distant conversations across Russia. Fears of suicide and of his mother's death pervaded his daily activities. By the spring of 1918, Chekhov's immediate family situation had deteriorated. His wife, Olga, divorced him, taking away their newborn daughter. Stanislavsky had a team of psychiatrists examine his overwrought, but still most popular, actor. Finally Chekhov underwent a series of hypnotic treatments, which eased the worst of his episodes of depression. Chekhov discovered, however, that he was subject to fits of uncontrollable laughter, which sometimes erupted in the middle of his stage performances.

More than the advanced psychological therapies of Stanislavsky's physicians, it was his encounter with Hindu philosophy and especially with Rudolf Steiner's Anthroposophy that altered Chekhov's psychic condition. In fact, Chekhov's passionate investigation of Steiner's "spiritual science" filled a dangerous void in his creative world. It unblocked his choking emotional life. Gradually, Chekhov understood that his maddening lack of will was the residue of a spiritual crisis rather than the physical fatigue of an overworked actor. Chekhov began to reason that his poorly timed breakdown—at the height of his fame—was actually his soul's silent protest against what he was becoming as a performer: "a malevolent vessel of drunken egotism." In many ways, Chekhov in 1918 resembled the Stanislavsky of 1905: both were praised as performers but intensely unhappy as individuals and artists. Both longed for a more perfect system of actor training, but

Chekhov also sought a more perfect style of communion with the audience. He dreamed of a new acting mode that contained a larger and deeper component, more akin to the ecstatic religiosity of the ancient Greeks than the petty commercialism and politics in the theatre of contemporary Russia.

During the war years, disciples of Rudolf Steiner, called Anthroposophists, performed private demonstrations of Eurythmy, or the "science of visible speech," in Moscow. These spiritual dances, which attempted to transform sound and color into movement, made a tremendous impression on Chekhov. Like the mantras and various yogas of Southeast Asia, Steiner's sound and movement exercises provided his followers with a sophisticated and clearly delineated artistic outlet. At Anthroposophical centers in Germany and Switzerland, performances that utilized Eurythmy—either as a new form of dance or as a basis for movement in Steiner's own Mystery Dramas—attracted a wide following. Although Chekhov did not meet with Steiner until 1922 during a Central European tour, his contacts with local Russian Anthroposophical groups were frequent and productive. More important, they stimulated Chekhov's ideas for an ideal theatre. Marrying the inner truth and emotional depth of Stanislavsky's System with the beauty and spiritual impact of Steiner's work became Chekhov's obsessive quest.

In 1918, Chekhov opened his own studio in the Arbat theatre district of Moscow. It was the first of several such attempts to pass on his singular form of acting. Of the hundreds of students who auditioned every autumn between 1918 and 1922, thirty were chosen each term. Normally only three remained by December. Chekhov rarely prepared a class. The Studio work emphasized his experiments in character development.

In his private flat, Chekhov at first investigated the concept of reincarnation and the techniques of Indian yoga. One novel exercise involved deep meditation. Tapping their minds' collective or racial unconscious, the students tried to become reincarnated as their characters. If a performer playing Hamlet, for instance, could somehow mentally metamorphose himself into the *actual* Hamlet, Chekhov felt a whole new chapter of actor training could be written.

Though few students, to be sure, shared Chekhov's personal beliefs and enthusiasm for the spiritual in his Studio, Chekhov invented a vocabulary that spoke more directly to the performer's thought process and imagination. Stanislavsky and Vakhtangov normally told actors what they wanted from them in abstract terminology, e.g., "to concentrate," "to act naively," "to feel heat." This caused the performer to reinterpret each command according to the workings of his mind and body. The instruction "to relax," for instance, a frequent directorial request, often produced a number of secondary responses in the actor's mind before physical relaxation could be achieved. An actor may think the following: "Although I feel relaxed, the director has said that I am not. Therefore, some part of my body must be tense. First I must determine where. I'll start with my shoulders. . . ."

Chekhov's Technique dealt primarily with images, especially visceral ones, that short-circuited complicated and secondary mental processes. Instead of telling the actor "to relax," Chekhov asked him "to walk [or sit or stand] *with a Feeling of Ease.*" The notion of "the Feeling of Ease" offered an outward, positive image for the actor and replaced Stanislavsky's directorial command "to relax." Another example: Rather than demand that a slouching performer who was playing a proud aristocrat "sit up straight," Chekhov told him to let his body *"think 'up.'"* While to the nonactor the differences between Chekhov's linguistic approach and that of his teachers may seem slight, for Chekhov they were crucial cues, showing a profound understanding of how the actor thinks and responds.

Both Chekhov and Stanislavsky believed that actors must

be given ways to go beyond the acting clichés and theatrical banalities that they inherited from older generations of established performers. For Stanislavsky, this meant that the actor had to look for "truth" in real human behavior or in the *logic* of human psychology. For Chekhov, the secret lay somewhere outside the theatre and life, somewhere deep in the performer's imagination. According to Chekhov's teachings, it was the stage's ineffable, magical elements that truly bring the actor and spectator together: the field of energy, or vitality, that radiates from the actor's creative work, his profound and startling character choices, the kinesthetic sensation of perfectly executed corporal movements and sounds—all create a special and powerful atmosphere, the pure atmosphere of the stage. The MAT's tired naturalism could be found everywhere in the streets, in daily life itself, so the theatre had no need to compete with that. Instead, Chekhov's challenge to Stanislavsky prophesied a new kind of performance style that used acting as a charged or otherworldly form of human communication.

More than anything else, Chekhov's work became associated with the power of the imagination. Since theatre's strength lies in its ability to communicate through sensory imagery rather than through literary ideas, Chekhov sought to uncover appropriate actor training devices that would heighten his students' imaginative awareness. His improvisations, which constitute the bulk of his early teachings, advanced the notion that scenic space could have a special, almost bewitching, aura filled with evanescent or intoxicating Atmospheres. Stanislavsky and Vakhtangov's Emotional Recall exercises were based on the actor's sensory memory of an *actual* event from his life. Chekhov schooled his students to find *fictional*, external stimuli from outside their personal experiences that could fire their emotions and imaginations.

During the start of Lenin's New Economic Policy period of limited capitalism (1921–27), the Chekhov Studio suffered financially. The productions of fairy tales and literary adapta-

tions that Chekhov and his students offered interested only
a limited audience. To survive, therefore, Chekhov was
forced to return to acting on the professional stage. Before
the demise of his studio in 1921, however, Chekhov played
a "trick" on Stanislavsky. Since starting his System, Stanislavsky had cautioned all his students and fellow teachers
never to reveal any details about their work. Although Stanislavsky had many critics outside the MAT, none could point
clearly to any single feature of his training because so little was
known about it. Only hearsay, rather than specifics, could be
reported and criticized. But in 1919 Chekhov published a
detailed analysis of Stanislavsky's work in two issues of the
workers' cultural journal, *Gorn* ("Crucible"). Stanislavsky
and the First Studio members were outraged—for two reasons: first, because Chekhov broke Stanislavsky's firm prohi-
bition, and second, because Chekhov mischievously at-
tributed some of his own extreme ideas to the master.

Two years later, however, both Stanislavsky and Vakhtangov forgave Chekhov. Early in 1921, Chekhov starred in
Vakhtangov's gloomy, expressionist production of August
Strindberg's *Erik XIV*. Playing the young and socially impo-
tent king of a corrupt Swedish court, Chekhov discovered the
character's internal nature in rehearsal by continuously
thinking of one startling image: Erik is trapped inside a circle.
His arms dart out of the circle, attempting to reach something. But Erik finds nothing. His hands are left hopelessly
dangling and empty. Inspired by the lessons of Eurythmy,
Chekhov "found" his role by playing with the shape and
quality of the character's movement and by rearranging his
physical stature and shape. Only when he "saw" the character's gesture did Chekhov begin his embodiment, or Incorporation, of the role. Using a purely external image, rather than
an Affective Memory, Chekhov created the character of Erik
in a non-Stanislavskian and striking manner.

Simultaneous with *Erik XIV*, Chekhov was rehearsing the
lead role in Gogol's *The Inspector General* for the Moscow Art

Theatre, under Stanislavsky's direction. The master director dominated his young performers, often stopping them midway through a sentence and then demonstrating his own personal acting choices. But Chekhov's private interpretation of Khlestakov was so unusual and his physical characterization so bold—"a malicious pixie from another world"—that even his First Studio companions were amazed. Stanislavsky did not try to improve upon Chekhov's choices.

On opening night of *The Inspector General*, a shocked Vakhtangov whispered to Stanislavsky, "Can this be the same man we see in our studio every morning?" Vakhtangov, who had been working with Chekhov on the *Erik XIV* project, now hardly recognized him in the Gogol character. Some spectators remarked that Chekhov brought a nuanced and strange lightness to the part. The sick, pathological, and flippant traits of Khlestakov perfectly and frightfully knitted themselves into a fresh interpretation. There is no doubt that Stanislavsky and others appreciated Chekhov's finished productions. What concerned the MAT crowd was Chekhov's erratic means of creating character. Every night his performance had a totally different feeling to it. His stage actions were improvised nightly. But more than that, Chekhov's character had a tendency to shift and refocus from performance to performance. It was as if Gogol's Khlestakov, once given life on stage, began to *direct* the actor Chekhov.

In 1923, after Vakhtangov's untimely death and the Moscow Art Theatre's celebrated tour of Western Europe and America, Stanislavsky rewarded Chekhov with the directorship of his own theatre, the Second Moscow Art Theatre. Freed of financial worries, Chekhov began to experiment in earnest. Exercises in rhythmic movement and telepathic communication filled the actors' crowded training and rehearsal schedules. For his final preparation for a controversial *Hamlet*, Chekhov taught his actors to use Shakespeare's language like a physical property, tossing balls as they rehearsed their lines. Chekhov announced to his cast, "If the System of K.S.

[Stanislavsky] is high school, then my exercises are university." Neither the actor's own personality nor stage clichés of a director or playwright were allowed to become the basis of any role. Chekhov claimed that his Hamlet varied from one performance to another, sometimes independent of his commands, in response to the unconscious needs of his audience. Some saw the Second Moscow Art Theatre's experimental production as a symbol of the Russian intellectual's political dilemma in the midst of the contemporary workers' state.

In the presentations that followed *Hamlet*, Chekhov demonstrated his legendary ability to transform himself from one physical type into another. For the Second MAT's production of *St. Petersburg* (1925), with its apocalyptic atmosphere based on Andrei Bely's Symbolist novel, Chekhov played the old Senator Abeleukov who refuses to believe that the old imperial order is about to collapse. Chekhov spoke of finding his archetype, or "correct" image, for the character in the movements and sounds of "loneliness." Although he seemed more a leading actor than an artistic director at the Second MAT, Chekhov's approach soon became the subject of severe government criticism. In Alexander Sukhovo-Kobylin's *The Case* (1927), he began to incorporate aspects of animals and supernatural beings into the physical embodiment of his character, Muromsky. In his preparation, Chekhov attempted to make "contact" with his vision of Muromsky, asking him questions and imitating his responses.

By 1927 Chekhov was officially denounced as an "idealist" and mystic because of his use of Eurythmy and his interest in Rudolf Steiner, now completely forbidden in Soviet culture. Protesting Chekhov's techniques, seventeen performers left the Second Moscow Art Theatre. Immediately following the split, the foremost Moscow newspapers branded Chekhov "a sick artist" and his productions "alien and reactionary." Within the year, he was marked for liquidation. But Chekhov's popularity and luck held. His work in film and the publication of his autobiography created support for him even within the government and the GPU, the Soviet domestic secret police. In August 1928, after receiving an invitation from the Austrian director Max Reinhardt to perform in Germany, Chekhov was given permission to emigrate with his family. He immediately left for Berlin. It was there that Chekhov began a second phase of his career, his *Wanderjahre*, "wandering years," a period that was of mixed professional and personal successes.

Arriving in Berlin in the late summer of 1928, Michael Chekhov started a second phase of his career, a voluntary exile across Central, Western, and Eastern Europe. For seven years, most of them filled with disappointments, Chekhov pursued outside Soviet Russia his lifelong quest to create his own troupe and method of actor training. But in every adopted country where his acting was highly praised, Chekhov's grandiose plans for a theatre studio or school stalled, backfired, or disintegrated. The traditional curse that plagued other Russian artists-in-exile—that no nation besides Mother Russia would fully embrace and understand them—doggedly pursued Chekhov wherever he went.

His first professional encounter abroad, with Max Reinhardt in Berlin, left Chekhov depressed and confused. Hoping to play a solo Hamlet on the German stage, Chekhov was cast instead as Skid, the brokenhearted husband of a rising Broadway starlet, in George Abbott's and Philip Dunning's Jazz Age play *Broadway*, retitled *Artists* in Europe. The play was already successful in Berlin, and Reinhardt arranged for a second production with Chekhov to be staged in Vienna. Now set in a circuslike arena in one of Vienna's largest theatres, *Artists* opened in February 1929. Everything about the production upset Chekhov: the short and sloppy rehearsal process, the general lack of direction, and, most of all, his own uninspired characterization. During the play's shaky premiere, however, a strange vision came to Chekhov: he saw the character Skid beckoning him to sit in a certain way, to speak in a new pitch, to move more slowly, to look with greater power at his wife. Chekhov interpreted this revelation in a personal and mystical way: "Fatigue and calm turned me into a spectator of my own performance. . . . My consciousness divided—I was in the audience, near myself, and in each of my partners." His acting in *Artists* was enthusiastically received, ensuring Chekhov a new career in the German-speaking world. Within one year he appeared in three major German films.

Chekhov called this visionary sighting Divided Consciousness, since it resulted in a dual awareness of performing before an audience while simultaneously following his character's guidance. In his last Soviet production, *The Case*, he had tried to conjure up the image of Muromsky. But only in Vienna did the character manifest itself naturally and fully. Obeying the Higher Ego, or stepping outside oneself to comply with the character's demands, became Chekhov's new credo. When Chekhov explained this concept to Stanislavsky later that spring in a Berlin café, the master became startled and perplexed. Furthermore, Chekhov admonished Stanislavsky for creating a harmful system of actor training, contending that Stanislavsky's heavy reliance on Emotional Recall devices led actors into uncontrolled hysteria. Suddenly their former pupil/teacher roles were reversed. Chekhov recommended that Stanislavsky replace Affective Memory with pure Imagination. Of the mind's three active phases (dreaming, thinking/remembering, and imagining), Chekhov lectured Stanislavsky, only imagination was truly effective in the creation of art. With the heat of Chekhov's passionate insistences Stanislavsky could only disagree.

In 1930, Vsevolod Meyerhold and other Soviet theatre artists visited Chekhov in Berlin, with the intention of persuading him to return to Moscow. Back in the Soviet Union, Meyerhold even joked to his actors about a plan to kidnap Chekhov. During this time, Chekhov himself was busy with Eurythmy and Anthroposophy, attending Rudolf Steiner centers in Germany. But also stranded in Berlin, in self-imposed exile from Russia and Palestine, were the Habima Players. They approached Chekhov, a fellow émigré from Russia and the MAT, and begged him to direct them in a Shakespeare play. Chekhov selected *Twelfth Night,* yet soon realized the youthful and overly serious disciples of Vakhtangov were anything but naturally comic performers. For them, Chekhov invented a series of Lightness exercises, which they attacked with their typically zealous fervor. By the time the play opened, the Hebrew *Twelfth Night* had a light, airy texture. Newspapers from around the world favorably reviewed the Habima's foray into Shakespeare. And Chekhov's reputation as an innovative director became known in France and the English-speaking world.

By early 1931, Chekhov began to think of leaving Berlin. He started work on a "compact" and modern-dress *Hamlet,* in which Claudius and Gertrude ingeniously played themselves and the Player King and Queen. Then several other projects were offered to Chekhov, like the directorship of two newly formed Russian-language theatres in Prague and Paris, but all of them collapsed financially. But Paris alone contained the largest Russian-speaking population outside the Soviet Union. In the spring of 1931, Chekhov made Paris his new home.

Pro- and anti-Bolshevik factions of the Russian émigré world in Paris joined forces to oppose Chekhov's theatre plans. Russian and French supporters of the Soviet Union viewed the nephew of Anton Chekhov as one more renegade bourgeois actor seeking material riches in the West; his repertoire eschewed contemporary politics, favoring nineteenth-century comedies and spiritual dramas. In addition, slighted that Chekhov refused to speak out against communism or sign their petitions, the powerful Russian anti-Bolshevik factions accused Chekhov of being an agent of the GPU. The few short evenings of Russian-language plays and sketches that Chekhov did mount in Paris did, however, find support

in the politically moderate French press. Still, technical im-
broglios and budgetary mismanagement complicated each
production.

With the financial assistance and producing skills of Georgette Boner, a young pupil of Max Reinhardt and founder of
the Deutsche Bühne Paris, Chekhov eventually established
his own theatre, the Chekhov-Boner Studio. In November
1931 it opened with a mystical pantomime created by and
starring Chekhov. It was based on Alexei Tolstoy's fairy tale,
The Castle Awakens. Concentrating on Symbolist-like decor
and musical effects as well as Eurythmic movement, Chekhov
hoped the production would attract a large international audience. Dozens of special exercises and etudes were created
to train his young actors. Wanting to avoid the problem of
performing exclusively before the Russian émigré community
or playing in badly accented French, Chekhov invented a
"universal language" for *The Castle Awakens,* using the ideas
of Rudolf Steiner. In fact, the sparse text consisted of only
fifty lines of fragmented dialogue—which, while "conceived"
in German, was performed in French.

Although the production was acclaimed by much of the
Parisian and foreign press, opening night difficulties with
the set and stagehands and the play's mystical theme damaged
the play's reception with the theatre-going public. Once
more, Chekhov's dream was failing. Highly sensitive to criticism, Chekhov never again experimented with the creation
of texts for his "future theatre." And after this experience,
Anthroposophy became a largely private concern in his life
and work.

Boner and Viktor Gromov, one of Chekhov's Russian
assistants, managed to secure positions for him at the state
theatres in the independent republics of Latvia and Lithuania
in 1932 and 1933. A handful of former First Studio and
Second Moscow Art Theatre members found their way to the
Baltic states and joined Chekhov's troupe. Now back in Eastern Europe, Chekhov briefly enjoyed stardom as both an

actor and master teacher. Performing in Russian, while the other actors played in their native languages, Chekhov finally overcame the linguistic barriers on stage that plagued his early wandering years. But the threat of war and a fascist coup, in addition to a growing xenophobia in the Baltic republics, sent Chekhov and his Russian colleagues temporarily back to Western Europe and then, at the invitation of the impresario Sol Hurok, to the United States.

Renamed the "Moscow Art Players" by Hurok, Chekhov's group opened a season on Broadway in the spring of 1935. Ignoring the diplomatic protests of the Soviet embassy in Washington, Hurok hoped that the Russian actors would be mistaken for the original Moscow Art Theatre. The deceptive name and advertising campaign proved to be unnecessary. Chekhov's eccentric characterizations and fine direction of Russian and Soviet classics took the American theatre intelligentsia by storm. A faction of the Group Theatre, led by Stella Adler, considered asking Chekhov to fill their newly vacated directorship. (Lee Strasberg and Cheryl Crawford had just resigned.) Adler, who had worked with Stanislavsky the previous year in Paris, remembered the master's dictate to seek out Chekhov wherever he might be performing. And now the stateless Chekhov had fallen into her hands. In response to the Group's pleading, Chekhov presented a lecture-demonstration on his Technique in September 1935. While Oliver Sayler, a noted authority on the Russian theatre who had seen Chekhov perform in *Twelfth Night* in Moscow, translated, Chekhov outlined the basic features of his teachings, especially as they related to characterization. The session was significant because it provided the first clearly stated examples of Chekhov's work since his exile from Moscow.

Chekhov declared that the end product of all actor training is the development of the stage character. He observed that the Stanislavsky actor has been taught to build his role on the similarities between his personal history and that of the character in the play. But this constant repetition of the actor's own nature in creating different parts over the years causes a progressive "degeneration of talent." The creative means are used less and less. Eventually, the actor will begin to imitate himself, relying, for the most part, on repeated personal mannerisms and stage clichés. Like Stanislavsky and Vakhtangov, Chekhov had touched on a fundamental problem of acting: the limited range of the standard actor's characterizations. But Chekhov's solutions, as outlined in the 1935 lecture, differed considerably from theirs.

Like Stanislavsky and the Moscow Art Theatre in Moscow, the Group Theatre was uncertain of how to react to Chekhov's explanation of his Technique. There were no doubts about Chekhov's extraordinary acting skills, but another question arose: Could his Technique be taught to others? Stella Adler and Bobby Lewis were excited about many of Chekhov's concepts. They would later utilize some of them in their own teachings. But most of the Group thought that Chekhov's theories were too extreme. Some left-wing members jokingly suggested that he be sent back to Russia.

Backstage after the Moscow Art Players' Broadway premiere, another young actress tried to get Chekhov's attention. This was Beatrice Straight. In her, Chekhov at long last found a sensitive and talented benefactor. With her friend Deirdre Hurst (soon to be Chekhov's secretary and editorial assistant), Straight invited Chekhov to Dartington Hall, the site of her family's estate and a progressive educational institution in Devonshire, England. In 1936, amid other experimental projects in agriculture, music, small-craft industry, and modern dance, Chekhov laid the foundation of his new theatre. There, in Dartington's utopian community (created nine years earlier by Straight's stepfather and -mother, Leonard and Dorothy Elmhirst), the trio of Chekhov, Straight, and Hurst recruited instructors and students to study the Chekhov Technique. Drawn from the United States, England, Canada, Australia, New Zealand, Germany, Austria, Norway, and Lithuania, two dozen young actors were to become the initiates of Chekhov's twenty-five-year-old dream, the Chekhov Theatre Studio. The training there was thorough and deliberate, lasting two full years.

In England, Chekhov turned much of the technical apparatus of the Stanislavsky System upside-down. As always, he was mostly concerned with the special physical nature of the actor's movement and the creation of new and exciting characters. Chekhov shared with Stanislavsky a belief in developing the actor's sources for inspiration, feeling, and expressiveness, but he taught that the stimulus should always begin *outside* the private and internalized world of the performer. At Dartington, simple exercises in "the Four Brothers" (the Feelings of Ease, Form, Beauty, and the Whole) schooled the performer in special psycho-physical movements, forcing him to think about his body in theatrical space as a choreographer or dancer would.

Chekhov's most radical innovation at Dartington was the further development of his substitutions for Stanislavsky's Sense Memory and Emotional Recall. Sensory stimulation came from the creation of Atmospheres and Qualities, or external expressions, which, when added to movement, provoked the feelings they mimed. To create, say, anger in a character, a student would be instructed only to "add the Quality of anger" to his gesture or movement rather than search for a past or internal motivation.

The marriage of Imagination, Atmospheres, and Qualities supplanted Stanislavsky's Affective Memory for Chekhov's students. For example, to awaken or capture the sensation of sadness, actors were told to do the following: (1) imagine the grieving sounds of a rural family mourning the accidental and gruesome death of a boy and a girl; (2) walk through the Atmosphere of a flood-devastated village; or (3) sit and stand with a "Quality of sadness." In this way Chekhov felt his performers could produce more powerful and individualized emotional expressions without having to consciously evoke difficult-to-control memories of personal experiences.

The Dartington period (1936–39) was a creative and happy time for the faculty and students, punctuated with high and intense artistic aspirations. Famous theatre and dance personalities, like Uday Shankar, visited the classes, but the creation of a professional theatre ensemble in England never materialized. There were other problems. Despite his mastery of English after only six months, Chekhov refused to perform on the British stage. Then, England's anticipation of war with Germany in 1939 caused the Chekhov Theatre Studio to cease operation and relocate across the Atlantic in Ridgefield, Connecticut, a rural community not far from New York City.

The bucolic conditions at the Ridgefield Studio in 1939 resembled those at Dartington Hall, yet its proximity to the New York theatre changed Chekhov's way of thinking about his school and means of instruction. First of all, the Studio felt its reputation would be enhanced with a successful New York production. So Chekhov, in cooperation with George Shdanoff, a friend and director, mounted a large-scale Broadway production of an adaptation of Dostoyevsky's *The Possessed*. They decided that studio actors—including newly recruited American ones—but not Chekhov himself would perform in it. Yet *The Possessed* neither demonstrated the Chekhov Theatre Studio's particular skills in acting nor its public relations abilities. It was compared, unfavorably, with the ensemble work of the Theatre Guild and Group Theatre. Few reviewers saw the effort as a new young American group's first theatrical endeavor. Had the hastily staged *The Possessed* succeeded, the Chekhov Technique might have found immediate and widespread support in the New York theatre community.

Shaken but not crushed by the commercial failure of *The Possessed*, the Chekhov Theatre Studio continued to undertake productions. Between 1940 and 1942, the Studio mounted three highly acclaimed and hugely ambitious seasons of classical plays and comedies. Performing in repertoire, the young actors toured outside New York City, to New

England, the Midwest, and the Deep South. Not since the days of traditional barnstorming theatrical tours in the teens and early twenties had most of the towns on their itinerary seen live and serious dramatic entertainment. The unusually high quality of the acting was noted in very nearly every county and city newspaper. A young and vibrant Yul Brynner played in the Studio's *King Lear.* This talented ensemble also included Hurd Hatfield and Beatrice Straight, with Ford Rainey in the lead. Yet that first Broadway fiasco haunted Chekhov. So he thought about bringing the Studio to New York in order to teach special classes for professional actors.

In the fall of 1941, a second Chekhov Theatre Studio opened on Fifty-sixth Street in New York. The transfer of emphasis to Manhattan brought Chekhov to a critical point in his long and unpredictable career. Was he primarily a teacher, actor, or director? It had been over a decade since Moscow and Berlin theatre critics had heaped praise on him as a performer. Yet Chekhov was determined to change the style of American acting. At his Studio Broadway actors could be retrained in his new Technique. There, Chekhov believed, he could directly influence the American theatre.

In addition to classes in the Chekhov Technique (conducted by Chekhov, George Shdanoff, Alan Harkness, Beatrice Straight, and Deirdre Hurst), a full curriculum of speech training, Eurythmy, music appreciation, choral singing, fencing, gymnastics, and makeup was offered at the Chekhov Theatre Studio in Manhattan. The twice weekly two-hour classes for professional actors, however, occupied a special place in Chekhov's thinking. Here he hoped to perfect and distill all the elements of his Technique, in particular those related to Psychological Gesture, his last and most widely discussed acting invention.

Chekhov believed that Psychological Gesture was the key to the actor's subconscious. A concentrated and repeatable movement or action, the Psychological Gesture awakens the actor's inner life, and its kinesthetic image feeds him while he acts on stage. Every character, according to Chekhov, possesses a single Psychological Gesture, which reveals his secret, innermost motivation and personality trait. Before doing anything else, the actor must unravel his character's Psychological Gesture. And through it, Chekhov wrote, the soul of the character and the physical body of the performer meet.

In October 1942, the Chekhov Theatre Studios disbanded because of the draft, which quickly absorbed most of the young male actors, and growing financial problems. With his wife, Xenia, Chekhov moved to Los Angeles, where he began a new career in American films. Between 1943 and 1954, Chekhov played character parts in nine Hollywood motion pictures. Basically, he was seen as a comic character or an eccentric East European type. In the film *Cross My Heart*, typically, Chekhov was cast as a mad Russian actor. Chekhov's character, in the role of Hamlet, has already killed one Claudius performer on stage and attempts to murder others unfortunate enough to be playing the King. In 1945, after receiving an Academy Award nomination for the role of the psychoanalyst in Alfred Hitchcock's *Spellbound*, Chekhov resumed teaching his Technique to young Hollywood actors. Marilyn Monroe, Jack Palance, Anthony Quinn, Mala Powers, John Dehner, John Abbot, and Akim Tamiroff were among his small cadre of students. On September 30, 1955, Chekhov, sixty-four, died of heart failure in his Beverly Hills home.

THE HISTORY OF THIS BOOK

Determined to promote the Chekhov Technique further, in 1941, Eugene Somoff, the Chekhov Theatre Studio's managing director, encouraged Chekhov to concentrate his efforts on completing a textbook on acting technique and style. Chekhov had written an autobiography in 1924 and a dozen or so articles for Soviet theatre journals and anthologies during the twenties, but only fragments of his thinking had appeared elsewhere. In 1931, at the Chekhov-Boner Studio in Paris, he'd begun work with Boner on a comprehensive writing project in German that would define his technique, but nothing publishable resulted from it. Beginning in 1935 at Dartington Hall into the final days of the Chekhov Theatre Studio seven years later, Deirdre Hurst (she married Edgard du Prey in 1942) kept a shorthand record of Chekhov's English-language lectures and exercise sessions. These transcriptions, numbering in the hundreds of pages, were to be the basis of Chekhov's text, *Michael Chekhov: To the Actor—Some New Ideas of Acting (with Exercises)*.

An introductory booklet by Chekhov was submitted to Dorothy and Leonard Elmhirst in 1937 at Dartington. They encouraged him to continue, and two years later, at Ridgefield, a fuller compilation of Chekhov's theories and work appeared in manuscript form. These first attempts were primarily a private means for him to solidify his thinking into a comprehensive system.

Finally, in 1942, Chekhov, with the assistance of two former students, Paul Marshall Allan and Hurd Hatfield, and Deirdre Hurst, completed a third, book-length, version of *Michael Chekhov: To the Actor.* In a letter to Deidre Hurst du Prey written from Hollywood on February 21, 1946, Chekhov said, "My English is as bad as always, and it was only my confidence in you—that you would understand me—which gave me the freedom to express myself without any inner difficulties." The Russian designer Nikolai Remisoff, a personal confidant, illustrated Chekhov's Psychological Gestures. Known as the "1942 version," it was submitted to several large publishing houses and influential editors in New York, as well as to sympathetic Hollywood agents. Citing wartime restrictions that severely rationed paper and press type, however, most of these readers, while intrigued by the subject, ultimately rejected it.

Blaming much of the failure of *Michael Chekhov: To the Actor* on his formal style of written English, Chekhov translated the text into Russian in 1945. It appeared one year later in a privately printed book, *O Tekhnike Aktera,* which Chekhov sent to American libraries and university Slavic departments at his own expense. Then he translated his Russian chapters back into English and resubmitted them to a number of American publishers, including Theatre Arts Books, which had profitably printed translations of Stanislavsky's works. But again, the "1942 version" was returned to Chekhov with encouraging letters and polite notices of rejection.

In 1952, Charles Leonard, a Hollywood producer and director, reedited Chekhov's manuscript, titled simply *To the Actor,* for Harper Brothers Publishers. The husband of Betty Raskin, Chekhov's manager and close friend, Leonard was given carte blanche by the ailing Chekhov. Greatly reduced in size and deleting much of Chekhov's spiritual and artistic explanations and examples, *To the Actor* provided the young postwar American performer with a streamlined and ahistorical approach to non-Method actor training. Unlike the Russian-language *O Tekhnike Aktera,* the Harper Brothers text received fine distribution and much attention in the theatre community. Moreover, a bookjacket endorsement by Gregory Peck and an introduction by Yul Brynner did much to popularize Chekhov's name and final reputation. Five years after Chekhov's death in 1955, Leonard reinserted some of Chekhov's missing scenic ideas and theatrical anecdotes in a compilation book entitled *Michael Chekhov's To the Director and Playwright* (Harper & Row: New York, 1963).

On the Technique of Acting is a slightly amended version of Chekhov's original 1942 text. It contains all the acting exercises and personal narrative that were excised from the 1953 *To the Actor.* A preface by Mala Powers and, as an afterword, her description of Chekhov's Hollywood classes have been added. A few paragraphs and a chapter on dramatic composition have been deleted, in part because it does not relate directly to Chekhov's teaching of acting, and in part because it appears verbatim in *To the Actor*. Some of Chekhov's written language and word choices have been altered to reflect his unique style of classroom presentation (as transcribed by Deirdre Hurst du Prey) rather than his intentionally formal mode of bookish instruction. *On the Technique of Acting* at last provides the reader with the true and practical voice of Michael Chekhov.

MEL GORDON
February 1991

MICHAEL CHEKHOV'S CHART FOR INSPIRED ACTING

By MALA POWERS

In 1949 I attended Michael Chekhov's classes for professional actors, which took place weekly at the home of the actor Akim Tamiroff in Beverly Hills, California. Before long I was studying privately with Chekhov as well. Once when I arrived at his home for my lesson, Mischa, as I had come to call him, gave me his hand-drawn "Chart for Inspired Acting," a rendition of which appears on page xxxvi. He told me that it was a kind of summary of his technique.

As Mischa stood in the center of his living room, he drew an imaginary circle around himself, explaining that the chart represented such a circle drawn around the actor. He asked

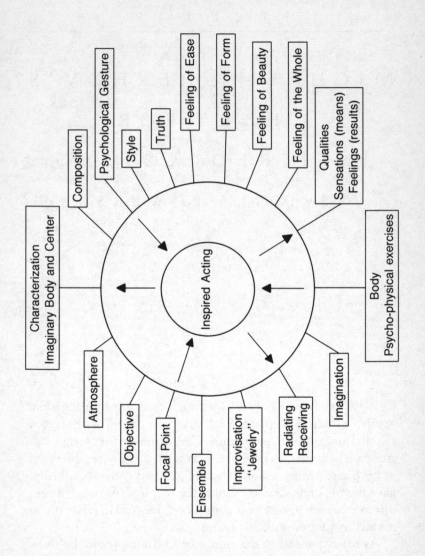

me to imagine that all the various techniques mentioned on the chart—Atmosphere, Characterization, Qualities, etc.—were like light bulbs on the circle's circumference. He said that when Inspiration "strikes," all the light bulbs are instantly turned on, illuminated.

"However, Inspiration cannot be commanded," Mischa insisted, "it is capricious. That is why the actor must always have a strong technique to fall back on."

Chekhov went on to explain that each one of the "light bulbs" is a point in the method—one of the components that is present in a truly great performance. When we exercise one point of the technique, "Atmosphere," for example, we can become so skillful in calling it up that the "Atmosphere light bulb" switches on. We learn to turn it on at will. Next, we exercise another point, for example "Radiating," until we become so powerful with this tool that the "Radiating light bulb" is illuminated. As we continue to master the various techniques in this way we soon find that we have only to consciously illuminate two or three light bulbs before a chain reaction begins and several more light up without our ever having to give them special attention. When a sufficient number of these light bulbs are shining brightly, we find that Inspiration strikes with much greater frequency than before.

The following summaries of various points of Michael Chekhov's Technique for actors may prove helpful, both to the student and as a kind of checklist for the professional actor.

CHARACTERIZATION (IMAGINARY BODY AND CENTER)

To create characters with physical features different from his own, the actor must first visualize an *Imaginary Body*. This Imaginary Body belongs to his or her character, but the actor can learn to inhabit it. Through constant practice, the performer can appear to change the length and shape of his body and physically transform himself into the character. Equally, every character has a *Center*. This is an imaginary area inside or outside the body where the character's impulses for all movement originate. The impulse from this Center initiates all gestures and leads the body forward or backward, and to sit, walk, and stand, etc. A proud character, for instance, can have a Center in his chin or neck, a curious character, one at the tip of his nose. The Center may be any shape or size, color, or consistency. A single character may even have more than one Center. Finding a character's Center can lead to understanding his or her entire personality and physical makeup. (See Chapters 4 and 6.)

COMPOSITION

In nature and art, there are mathematical laws and principles that structure and balance form. This feeling for *Composition* creates contours and prevents the expression of ideas, dialogues, movements, colors, shapes, and sounds from being nothing more than a flattened-out accumulation of impressions and events. The sense of Composition guides the artist and the spectator into the sphere of creativity and understanding. (See Chapter 8.)

PSYCHOLOGICAL GESTURE

This is a movement that embodies the psychology and Objective of a character. Using the actor's entire body, and executed with the utmost intensity, it gives the actor the basic structure of the character and at the same time can put the actor into the various moods required by the script. (See Chapter 5.)

FEELING OF STYLE

Everything on the stage is unreal. An actor working with a *Feeling of Style* attempts to capture the special nature of a play, screenplay or scene, rather than strive for a superficial sense of "reality." Tragedy, drama, melodrama, farce, comedy, and clowning are stylistic categories or modes that require separate and precise experiences. (See Chapter 7.)

FEELING FOR TRUTH

This is a question of "opening" yourself—developing your sensitivity to truthful behavior while acting. There are several facets of truth. (1) Individual or psychological truth: "My movements and my speech are true to myself, to my psychology." (2) Being true to the given circumstances of the script. (3) Historical truth: When playing period plays, do not overlook the sense of style of the age. Also, penetrate the style of the nation where the action takes place. (4) Stylistic truth: Experience the style of the play—tragedy, comedy, farce, drama, etc. Also, learn to experience other nuances of style in addition to those categories of theater—Brechtian, Shakespearean, etc. (5) Being true to the character. This will differ with every role. The character dictates it, and you must become more and more receptive to what the character is showing you about itself. (6) The truth of relationship: The often subtle differences and attitude of one character to each of the other characters around him.

FEELING OF EASE

This is a rich alternative to Stanislavsky's relaxation technique. As a directive, it produces immediate sensations and visceral imagery in the actor and avoids the intellectual, conscious process of interpreting a command. For instance, the actor can be asked "to sit with a *Feeling of Ease*," rather than "to relax." The actor can quickly perform the first command but must stop and *think* about the second one. (See Chapter 4.)

FEELING OF FORM

The actor must be sensitive to the form of his or her own body as well as to his own movement through space.

Like a choreographer or sculptor, the actor molds bodily forms. When the actor awakens this feeling for his body's form and sculptural movement, it enhances his ability to influence his body in the most expressive ways. This special awareness is called the *Feeling of Form*. (See Chapter 4.)

FEELING OF BEAUTY

Within each artist, often deeply hidden, is a wellspring of living beauty and harmony of creation. Becoming aware of this inner beauty of being is a first step for the actor who can then allow this beauty to permeate all his or her expressions, movements, and characterizations—even the "ugly" ones. Beauty is one of the outstanding qualities that distinguishes all great works of art. (See Chapter 4.)

THE FEELING OF ENTIRETY (OR THE WHOLE)

An artistic creation must have a finished form: a beginning, a middle, and an end. Equally, everything on the stage or screen should convey this sense of aesthetic wholeness. This *Feeling of the Whole* is strongly felt by an audience and must become second nature to the performer. It can apply to an entire production, a scene, or a single monologue. (See Chapter 4.)

QUALITIES (SENSATIONS AND FEELINGS)

Feelings cannot be commanded, they can only be coaxed. The means for coaxing up Feelings are Qualities and Sensations. Qualities are immediately accessible to you— especially to your movements. You can immediately move your arms and hands with the *Quality* of tenderness, joy, anger, suspicion, sadness, impatience, etc., even though you do not experience the Feeling of tenderness, joy or anger. After moving with one of these qualities, sooner or later you will observe that you are experiencing the

Sensation of tenderness, and very soon this Sensation with call up a true emotion or *Feeling* of tenderness within you. (See Chapter 3.)

BODY (PSYCHO-PHYSICAL EXERCISES)

The human body and mind are inseparable. No work of the actor is completely psychological nor exclusively physical. The physical body of the actor (and character) must always be allowed to influence the psychology and vice versa. For this reason, all of the actor's exercises must be psycho-physical and not executed in a mechanical fashion. (See Chapter 6.)

IMAGINATION

Nearly all acting is the result of the performer's ability to Imagine and reproduce the reality of the play's fiction on stage or screen. The more an actor can stimulate and train his Imagination and fantasy life, the greater will be his or her power to communicate the depth and meaning of the character. (See Chapter 1.)

RADIATING/RECEIVING

Radiating is the ability to send out the invisible essence of whatever quality, emotion, or thought you wish. It should be sent with great strength. Radiating is an activity of your "Will." You may even consciously "radiate" your character's presence onto the stage or set before you make an entrance. The "charisma" of an actor or actress on stage or screen corresponds to the degree of purely invisible radiation he or she is able to achieve. Some people have this ability naturally, others need to spend a good deal of time "Radiating" in order to develop it.

Receiving has just as strong an effect as Radiating, but instead of "sending out" Qualities, Thoughts, and Feelings, the character "pulls them in" from other characters, from Atmospheres, from the audience, from everywhere.

The actor must develop the ability to do this with great strength, just as with Radiating. It is valuable for you to ask of each character you are playing, "Are you principally a "Radiating character" or a "Receiving character"? Bear in mind that "Radiating characters" will switch to strong "Receiving" in some scenes and vice versa. (See Chapter 4.)

IMPROVISATION AND "JEWELRY":

In addition to using improvisation in preparatory work, Chekhov suggested that Improvising is also valuable during the final stages of work on a part. After your scaffolding is built—your characterization established, your lines, sequences of business, and emotional sections firmly memorized—improvise once more. Paraphrase the lines or ignore them altogether, perhaps allowing your character to speak the "subtext" (what he or she is *really* thinking). Use modified business or entirely different business and pay special attention to "how" your character is fulfilling this business. Notice all the things your character is aware of, what he sees or hears or pays momentary attention to while the scene is progressing. Rehearsing invented activities will make it much easier to develop the *"Jewelry"* in your performances—nuances and little shining moments of uniqueness that are memorable and that delight both you and the audience.

ENSEMBLE

Theatre is a collective art. The way one develops a performance in rehearsal is almost always manifested in production. When actors are artistically open and tuned in to each other, the total theatrical experience for artist and audience is heightened. Atmospheres become more powerful, the relationship between characters is stronger and more clearly defined, even the actor's "timing" and the rhythm of scenes becomes more fluid and alive. A sense of *Ensemble* also allows the actors to radiate a feeling of artistic control and to convey the power of the human spirit. (See Chapter 7.)

FOCAL POINT

Not everything going on within a scene is of equal importance. Generally the director should be in charge of the *Focal Point* (what he or she wants the audience to focus on at any given time), but the actor should also become aware of the most important moments in a script. The actor must know which moments are most important for his own character. *How* the actor focuses the attention of the audience on those moments is a truly creative task. The actor may choose to communicate it to the audience by subtly stressing (or Radiating) a gesture or by the lift of an eyebrow, rather than by stressing or relying upon the spoken line. A pause or a tiny unexpected jerk of the shoulders may also create the Focal Point and garner the audience's attention for the desired communication. (See Chapter 7.)

OBJECTIVE

This is the purpose or goal toward which your character is striving. Each character has both an *Objective* and a *Super-Objective.* An example of a Super-Objective might be "I want to serve humanity." An example of the Objective might be "I want to keep peace among these particular people." Ideally, all Objectives should begin with "I want to . . ." followed by an "actable" verb. (See Chapter 7.)

ATMOSPHERE

Atmospheres are sensory mediums, like fog, water, darkness, or confusion, that permeate environments and Radiate from people. On stage, the heightened mood of Atmospheres fills the theatre; both performer and spectator are unconsciously affected as an atmosphere's unseen waves are absorbed by the actor and Radiated out to the audience. Although they cannot be seen, Atmospheres can be felt strongly and are a primary means of theatrical communication. The Atmosphere of a Gothic cathedral, a hospital, or a cemetery influences anyone who enters those spaces. They become enveloped in the Atmosphere. People also give off personal Atmospheres of tension, hate, love, fear, foolishness, and so forth. The play or the director suggest the Atmosphere of a scene and the performers work together to create and maintain it; they are in turn influenced by it. (See Chapter 3.)

1

IMAGINATION AND CONCENTRATION

*Man feels himself younger and younger,
the more he enters into the world of
imagination. He knows now that it was
only the intellect which made him
stiff and aged in his soul expression.*
RUDOLF MEYER

THE CREATIVE IMAGINATION

At night when we are alone in our bedrooms, sharp images often emerge from the darkness. Before our mind's eye the events of the day mysteriously appear. The faces of people we have seen, their conversations and mannerisms, the streets of a city or the fields of the countryside suddenly reveal themselves. Mostly, we look passively at these familiar pictures, but among them appear strange visions, unknown to us. Scenes, moods, events, and people with which we have no connection intermingle with our everyday mental images and branch out in all directions. The new images seem to develop and transform themselves independent of our control or wishes. And when this occurs, we are drawn into another realm.

We may discover ourselves pursuing some mysterious phantom, solving nonexistent problems, or traveling in a foreign country, speaking with strangers, seeing the fantastic arising from nowhere, often beckoning, sometimes repelling. We watch things happen; we "spy" on whole situations that grow from nothing. As the curious images become stronger and stronger, they lead us sometimes into laughter or tears, into joy or sorrow. The whole range of our feelings finally is aroused.

Glimpses of this unfamiliar terrain lead us to believe that our images have a certain existence of their own—that they come from another world. This is even apparent when we train ourselves to perform conscious work upon our creative imagination. Artists in every field affirm that such images surround them not only after the day is over, when solitude and night come, but also during the day, when the sun shines, in the noisy city or in a small room—everywhere. Artists live with their images. They and their images belong to each other, depend upon each other, and yet the images have an independent existence of their own.

The great German director Max Reinhardt confessed, "I am always surrounded by images." Charles Dickens wrote in his journal, "I have been sitting here in my study all morning, waiting for Oliver Twist who has not yet arrived!" Goethe declared that inspiring images must appear before us as God's children and call to us, "We are here!" Raphael saw an image moving within his room that later became the Sistine Madonna on his canvas. Michelangelo complained despairingly that images pursued him and forced him to sculpt in all sorts of materials, even solid rock.

How can we question the beliefs of these master artists and writers that their imaginative life came to them from outside themselves? And would they not scorn the narrow conception of creativity that relies solely upon personal memories and efforts? They would undoubtedly feel that today we deny our communication with the objective world of imagination, in direct contrast to their free excursions into it. The creative impulse of the masters was an expansion toward the world beyond them, while ours is often a contraction within ourselves.

The old masters of European and Asian culture might even shout to us, "Look at your creations. They are not confined to reproductions of our petty, personal lives, desires, and limited surroundings. Unlike the artists of today, we forgot our individual selves in order to be conscious and active servants of otherworldly images. Truly, we did not want to be slaves to these unguided visions. But in our work, we incorporated them like an unexpected blessing. Why are you then creating so many specimens of ugliness, disease, and chaotic contortions? Is it not simply because you are too concerned with yourselves alone and not your art?"

The conviction that there is an objective world in which our images lead their independent life widens our horizon and strengthens our creative will. Developing and assuming new conceptions concerning the creative process in art is the way for the artist to grow and to understand his or her talent. One of these new conceptions is the objective existence of the world of the artist's creative images. What is the reward of artists brave enough to acknowledge the objectivity of the world of the imagination? They free themselves from the constant pressure of their too personal, too intellectual interference with the creative process, the greater part of which is intensely personal and takes place in the sphere that lies beyond the intellect.

TO WAIT ACTIVELY

Great artists of the past and the present, in acknowledging the innate laws governing the imagination, also accept the necessity of waiting patiently until the image has matured to its highest expressiveness. Leonardo da Vinci waited years before he could envision the head of Christ in his "Last Supper," and Goethe tells us that he bore the idea for one of his works with him for forty years before it was ripe for expression. Such a protracted period of time is, of course, impractical for the artist of today, yet in principle, it is an admonition to modern actors who, in their haste, have lost touch with their imagination and consequently with the ripeness of its images.

CREATIVE "GAZE"

Let us not suppose that this necessity to wait, to pause inwardly before the image, is a passive state. On the contrary, the truly awakened imagination is in constant, fiery activity.

What did the great masters of the past do while observing the ripening of their images? They collaborated with them through their fiery "gaze," their creative, urging attention. They saw what they wanted to see, and in this lay the power of their "gaze," but they also enjoyed the independent activity of their images, which transformed themselves under their questioning look, acquiring new qualities, feelings, desires, manifesting novel situations, symbolizing new ideas, revealing fresh rhythms. Thus they worked consciously hand in hand with their images. (We shall discuss the proper way to question your images in Chapter 6.)

TO "SEE" THROUGH THE IMAGES

For artists with mature imaginations, images are living beings, as real to their minds' eyes as things around us are visible to our physical eyes. Through the appearance of these living beings, artists "see" an inner life. They experience with them their happiness and sorrows; they laugh and cry with them and they share the fire of their feelings.

Look, for instance, upon such creations as King Lear on the heath, or King Claudius in the chapel. Shakespeare, watching these images, must have witnessed in them an intense emotional storm. Michelangelo, when creating his "Moses," must have been overwhelmed by the inner power of his image to force the medium of stone to such an effortless pitch. Not only did he "see" the muscles and sinews, the folds of cloth, the waves of hair and beard of his "Moses," but he "saw" before his mind's eye the inner might that molded all the muscles, folds, and waves in their rhythmical interplay. Why would Leonardo da Vinci have once exclaimed, "Where there is the most intense power of feeling, there is the greatest martyr," if he himself had not been burned by the fiery life of his images?

This inner life of the images, and not the personal and tiny experiential resources of the actor, should be elaborated on the stage and shown to the audience. This life is rich and revealing for the audience as well as for the actor himself. Ethel Boileau wrote, "You will see images as in a vision mirrored in your imagination. You will give them form, substance and reality, but you will never know quite whence they come. They are greater than yourself—and when you see them manifest a symbol, they will have a life of their own which is not your life—a mind which is not the reflection of your own. It is then that you will ask yourself, 'What is this that I have brought into being?' And the profounder their meaning and significance, the more you will question."

KNOWLEDGE THROUGH IMAGES

The acceptance of this independent world of imagination, the ability to penetrate through the outer appearance of the vision into its inner, fiery life, the habit of waiting actively until the image is right, brings the artist to the verge of discovering new and hitherto hidden things. Undoubtedly the image of "Moses" brought new creative insight to Michelangelo. " 'Parsifal' occupies me very much," wrote Richard Wagner, "namely, a peculiar creature, a fascinating world-demoniac woman, always livelier, appears before me." This is the process of acquiring new knowledge through the imagination. Through painting "The Last Supper," surely da Vinci increased his divine understanding and thus put forth his private philosophy that "good men" always seek knowledge.

This longing for knowledge makes the real artist brave. He never adheres to the first image that appears to him, because he knows that this is not necessarily the richest and more correct. He sacrifices one image for another more intense and expressive, and he does this repeatedly until new and unknown visions strike him with their revealing spell.

Poor indeed is the imagination that leaves the artist's mind cold, and poor indeed is the influx of wisdom to such an artist, when one hears him say, "I have built my art upon my convictions." Would it not be better for an artist to say that he has built his convictions upon his art? But this is only true of the artist who is really gifted. Haven't we noticed that the less talented the person is, the earlier he forms his "convictions" and the longer he tenaciously clings to them?

DEVELOPING THE SENSE OF TRUTH

The more the artist develops his ability to imagine, the more he comes to the conclusion that there is something in this process that somehow resembles the process of logical thinking. He sees more and more that his images follow with a certain inner regularity, although they remain entirely free and flexible. They become, in Goethe's words, "exact fantasy."

It is of great importance for the actor to develop a kind of "instinct," which will show him where to deviate from the sound "logic" of his images. Thinking and reasoning alone will not help him—the sense of truth is the principle that counts. This sense has been lost in our time, but it can be developed again. Perhaps it will take a long time for the actor to discover noticeable results in himself, but the way itself is a simple and pleasant one. The creations of great masters of the past can again render us their kind service and help us achieve these results.

EXERCISE 1.

Look at any classical architectural forms of different styles. Reproductions will do for this purpose. Study them. Follow their lines, forms, dimensions; try to experience their weight, the interplay of the powers of gravity in them. Study the connections between separate parts of the whole architectural form. Try to guess their function, whether it be to support, to lift, to suspend, and so forth. What is the main character of the whole? Is it stressing upward, does it cover and protect, is it inclined to remain near the ground, does it want to vibrate, to fly away, to spread itself, to contract? You do not need to study any professional books on architecture for such an exercise—it is even better if you do it freely and intuitively. Thus you will find many ways to penetrate deeply into the architectural form and to experience it. But most of all, enjoy its beauty. Then, after having become a good friend of the whole thing, suddenly ask yourself, "How would it look if this pillar were twice as thin as it is, if the tower were three times lower, the arch became square, the roof flat, the window broad?" And so on. From such questioning you will receive a shock, sometimes even a humorous one!

You can do something similar with classical sculpture and painting by trying to change the forms and colors.

EXERCISE 2.

Then go to Shakespeare's works, and after reading or studying one of his dramas, ask yourself some basic questions concerning the play's plot. For instance, ask yourself how it would be if Othello, in the middle of the play, suddenly understood that Iago had deceived him? What if the performance that Hamlet arranges in the castle should make no impression on Claudius? What if Olivia, in *Twelfth Night*, were really deeply depressed by her brother's death? Ask yourself many such questions.

EXERCISE 3.

The best material for developing a good sense of artistic truth is offered in authentic folk or fairy tales. They depict destinies, suffering, heroism, downfalls, growth and development, mistakes, inner defeats, and final victories of individuals and mankind. They are true human psychology, true history, and they prophesy in tragic and humorous pictures. Their source was never a purely aesthetic or poetic one. Fairy tales have their concrete "logic" because they arise from the time when the wisdom of humanity was fixed in the images and symbols that we find in fairy tales. They are not arbitrary because they were seen by the ancients as the outer expression of inner truth and wisdom. Rudolf Meyer expressed this elegantly: "The fairy tale and its ancient motifs comes through the rise and fall of people, and through the rise and fall of different world-outlooks."*

Read or recreate a fairy tale, but do not ask questions as before. The images and events will of their own volition work in your creative subconscious, gradually implanting a sense of truth in you.

Now, if you feel yourself advanced enough in this

---

*Rudolf Meyer (b. 1896) was a popular German philosopher during the twenties and an art historian associated with German Romanticism and Indian art.

way, read the biographies of notable people. Follow their destinies by imagining their lives. Let their destinies live in you for days and even weeks. The wisdom of it will continuously increase and refine your sense of truth.

You mustn't say that you do not believe in an objective wisdom interfering with human fate. As a private person you may or may not believe it, but as an artist, as an actor, you have to accept this point of view. On the stage you have to deal with the destinies of your characters, and if you want to play a character in a fine, masterly way, you must conceive it as a panorama of destiny.

You would do well to continue such exercises until you discover that images which are accidentally and arbitrarily put together react upon you as tasteless and amateurish productions.

CONCENTRATION

How can the actor keep his grasp firmly on the turbulent world of fiery images? From where shall he take the strength to fix these movable, flexible images? The ability to concentrate his attention to the highest degree—that is his strength. Every one of us has the ability to concentrate. All of us use it constantly—we cannot even cross the street without it. For the creative process, however, it is not enough to use this everyday degree of concentration. Keep in mind that there is no limit to the extent to which this power can be developed.

EXERCISE 4.

Start by looking at an object. Describe it to yourself inwardly. Is it broad and low? Is it long and high? Is it of wood or metal? Is it fluid, static, or mobile? Concentrate your attention on it. Try to acquire continuity of attention. As you concentrate do not miss any qualities or details. Certain gaps or distractions will appear to undermine your concentration. Firmly avoid them and continue.

Then do the same with an audible object.

EXERCISE 5.

Then concentrate on any known thing (an object or a sound) that you remember but that is not perceptible at the moment of the exercise. Apply the same conditions as you did before.

Now imagine and concentrate on fantastic objects: flowers, beings, landscapes, abstract forms, and so on.

Imagine noises, for instance wind, storm, waves, crowded streets, factories, melodies, voices, spoken words and sentences, and concentrate on them.

Try to imagine fantastic sounds.

EXERCISE 6.

Concentrate again on the same objects, first visible and then imaginary. This time inwardly embrace the object. As fully as possible, grasp the object as though with "invisible hands." Send out your whole inner being toward it. Experience your connection with the object in your arms, legs, torso. Let your whole being, as it were, participate in this embrace. This will lead you to a sense of merging with the object. At the same time, release any physical tension that may arise. Concentration is an inner event. Remain free and unstrained in your body, your eyes, your face, and even your brain.

EXERCISE 7.

Proceed with all the above-mentioned exercises in the following way. When you feel that the contact with the object is firmly established, when it has been "grasped" and held by you in your "invisible hands," begin to do things that have no relation to the object of your concentration. Start to move things in the room, to speak with somebody, to find a hidden thing, to open a certain page in a book, and so forth. While doing so try to maintain the inner bonds that connect you with the object of your concentration.

During such exercises you may have similar experiences to those you have had when waiting concentratedly for days for somebody to come or something to happen, while the ordinary trend of your life followed its own course without interruption.

The actor who can concentrate well makes a stronger impression upon the audience because all his acting becomes clearly shaped, sure, and explicit. Vagueness disappears in his behavior on the stage, and his presence on the boards grows more and more impressive.

I remember a gala performance-demonstration in Konstantin Stanislavsky's own home, given before a selected audience in a festive atmosphere. Among the chairs was one in the middle, waiting for a distinguished guest whom Stanislavsky had chosen to honor specially. But the guest was delayed and the performance could not begin. Impatiently Stanislavsky looked at the curtain; his whole attention was focused on the preparations going on behind it, while toward the rest of his surroundings he was naturally distracted. Suddenly a happy smile flashed over the face of the white-haired master. With outstretched arms he rushed toward the crowded door and led the guest to the chair, forced him, in spite of his humble protests, to accept the place of honor, and gave the sign for the curtain to be raised. All eyes were turned toward the chair in which sat a little man—the chauffeur of the long-expected guest!

With his mind so concentrated on the performance, Stanislavsky had completely forgotten that the honored guest was not a man at all, it was a lady! Such a price was often paid by Stanislavsky for his extraordinary power of concentration. Therefore, don't do your exercises on concentration while walking along the street!

IMAGINATION AND CONCENTRATION

The more we are able to sustain a strong bond of concentration with visible and invisible objects to which we direct our attention, the closer we will approach an understanding of the nature of real imagination. The following exercises will combine practice in both concentration and imagination.

FLEXIBILITY OF IMAGES

The flexibility of our images is one of their most important qualities. These images must be able to influence and lead each other, to change themselves, merge with each other, to follow their own logic freely, inspiring, suggesting, and enriching us at the same time.

EXERCISE 8.

Imagine events of mobility and transformation: a castle transforming under a spell, a poor beggar woman turning into a witch, a princess becoming a spider, a young person slowly aging and vice versa, a seed growing into a tree, a winter landscape changing into a summer one, and so on. Do not skip any of the stages of transformation.

The next exercise will help you to develop the ability to wait actively, as we have described before.

EXERCISE 9.

Choose any episode in a fairy tale. Imagine it fully. Leave it until the following day, then return to the imaginary episode. After such a period of secret growth, the images will have moved on to new situations, fresh inner attitudes, bringing with them new contributions from their own world. Now look for more complicated, more detailed fulfillment. Before putting the images aside, set before them definite tasks, such as: show more characteristics; show more development in a good or evil way; become older; become younger; become more passionate or calm; reveal the costume, the inner attitude, the kind of movement. These questions are arbitrary. Then return to the images on the third day, the fourth, and so on, prompting them to fulfill more and more tasks.

The images of this exercise pass through two phases: the first, in which they are directly influenced by your creative "gaze," and the second, in which they develop independently with your assistance.

DISCARD FIRST IMAGES

It must be remembered that courage is needed to discard first images and to resist being too easily satisfied. What has already been found will never be lost, but will be transformed and purified in one's subconscious. Thus the standard of the actor's imagination will grow and with it a love for completion, in which actors of our time are so lacking. It will also become a great stimulus for the imagination to reveal to us new and unknown things.

EXERCISE 10.

Choose any character from a play or fairy tale. Elaborate it in your imagination as clearly as possible. Then discard it and start from the beginning, trying to make it more complete, expressive, and original.

You must be very familiar with the play or fairy tale from which you have taken your image, otherwise you will not have the guiding motive with which to improve it. The completion of the image must be measured from the point of view of the whole play or fairy tale to which it belongs. Having discarded your first image, do not force it to disappear completely—this is impossible and unnecessary. Such an effort might even interfere with your attempt to create a second, better, image. The first image will disappear slowly, and perhaps completely, as the second one grows. Usually the first image leaves with the second its best features. Go on discarding one image after another in this way, as long as you feel inner satisfaction from this exercise. Then take another image. Do this intensively but unhurriedly for many days.

After you have achieved a certain skill in discarding and improving images, try to create an original image, real or fantastic. Work with it in the same way you have with previous images. In this instance you will have a different criterion for the improvement of the image. Before, you had the play or fairy tale by which to judge whether the image was truly complete, while now you have to improve it according to your own conception of it. You may be unaware of the full details of your conceived idea, but you will feel that it is your artistic taste urging you to change the image in this or that direction.

2

THE
HIGHER
EGO

*When I was very young I used
to say "I"; later on I said
"I and Mozart"; then "Mozart
and I"; now I say "Mozart."*
CHARLES GOUNOD

Our artistic natures have two aspects: one that is merely sufficient for our ordinary existence and another of a higher order that marshals the creative powers in us. By accepting the objective world of the imagination, the independent interplay of our images, and the depth of the subconscious activity in our creative lives, we open up the very limited boundaries of our "personalities." We confront the Higher Ego.

Both of these two functions are clearly perceptible in a developed artist. How often is his day-to-day life unexpectedly simple, in contrast to his professional life in which he is an exceptional individuality. Anton Chekhov collected one-kopek coins with the utmost seriousness; Maxim Gorky could not stand people looking at him; I saw Stanislavsky obsessively dusting chairs, tables, and shelves in his apartment, without any apparent necessity for it; Yevgeny Vakhtangov played simple tunes on the mandolin for hours, without ever achieving any great heights in this art.

But the usual ego is not what stirs our imagination. It is the other, the Higher Ego, the artist in us that stands behind all our creative processes. The more an artist recognizes this higher function in himself, the more he is influenced by it in his creative work. To turn our consciousness upon it, to see the concreteness of its specific powers and qualities, is a means of strengthening our connection with it. Let us therefore discuss four main ways in which our Higher Ego can influence our practical artistic work.

CREATIVE INDIVIDUALITY

Suppose a group of painters sat before the same landscape with their paints, and each promised himself faithfully to record the view before him. What would be the result? Several entirely different pictures would emerge. Why is this so? Because the artists did not paint the landscape, but their own individual conception of it, one made possible by each painter's Creative Individuality. They painted exactly the same subject, but they did not render the landscape that they saw outwardly; they painted the landscape within themselves. The voice of each artist's Creative Individuality inspired his particular interpretation. Their pictures will tell us that one of them was more charmed by the atmosphere of the landscape, another by the beauty of the form and line, the third by the language of contrasts, and so on.

"How often has *Iphigenia* been written and still each interpretation is different," wrote Goethe, "and this is because each sees and expresses the thing differently in accordance with this artistic perception." The same is true of the stage. We often hear it said, for instance, that there is only one Hamlet—the one that Shakespeare created. But who knows what Shakespeare's Hamlet was? The actor who venerates Shakespeare and reproduces his characters exactly, without individual deviations, may become like the musician who idolized Beethoven to such an extent that he finally ceased to play his music because he was afraid of an inexact reproduction of Beethoven's ideas. The actor will more adequately express his reverence for Shakespeare if he allows the spark of his individual fire to be kindled by Shakespeare's flame, instead of sycophantically and coolly "obeying" him by giving an impersonal recitation of Shakespeare's text from the stage.

I once revealed to a celebrated Russian writer my theatrical conception of considering Hamlet's destiny as being enclosed between two worlds. Starting with the meeting of the spirit of his father, when his sole attitude is directed toward a higher being and an unknown world, Hamlet finishes by looking downward into the grave, meditating on the nothingness of human existence. How exciting it would be to follow the composition of the events of Hamlet's destiny, enclosed in the frame of these two polarities! The famous writer asked, ironically, "Do you think that Shakespeare was of your opinion?" There is no answer for this dry, intellectual point of view. With all modesty the actor must have his own approach to what he is going to create.

On another occasion, I observed the psychology of an actor who was constantly drawn to evil, negative characters. Strangely enough, the more expressively he performed them, the more sympathetic they became, remaining nevertheless unmistakably evil. His secret became clear when I understood that the basic aim of his Creative Individuality was to vindicate the human condition. Speaking of a French poet, Goethe maintained, "He has found common recognition, not because of his poetic value, but because of the greatness of his character, which stands out from all his writings. The style of the writer," he continued, "is a true expression of his Inner Being." The same note is heard when Goethe spoke of Shakespeare as "a being of the higher order."

This aim of our Creative Individuality is not to be confused with propaganda, which is a preconceived and schematically devised and fixed expression. This confusion can lead to such extremes in the theatre as one Soviet production of *Hamlet,* which ridiculed the idea of monarchy, court, and aristocracy. Hamlet was played as a brutal, dirty lad with crown askew and a squalling pig under his arm, while Ophelia was a drunken prostitute. But the true voice of the Creative Individuality does not normally lead one to approach each complicated part with the "idea" of performing the hero "just as I am in my everyday life," whether the character be Faust, Lear, Hamlet, or any other. This is a way of simply avoiding *any* approach to the problem.

Freeing and stimulating our Creative Individuality can be helped by exercises such as the following:

EXERCISE II.

Study a character that you think you could act until you are familiar with it. Then try to imagine it as performed by different actors whom you know well. Observing the acting of the same part by different Creative Individualities, try to see wherein lies the difference in their acting. What features of the character become more marked in each of these cases? Which is more sympathetic? Which less? And so on. You will gradually learn to see the Creative Individualities of the actors through the mask of the character.

Conclude this exercise by acting the same part yourself in your imagination. Here you will experience something like a meeting with your own Creative Individuality, as a contrast to all others. Remember not to analyze your Creative Individuality. Confine yourself to experiencing it.

<u>**EXERCISE 12.**</u>

Choose some very simple business, like cleaning a room, finding a lost article, setting the table. Repeat this action at least twenty or thirty times. Each time avoid repetition of any kind. Do each action in a new way with a fresh inner approach. Keep only the general "business" as a spine for the exercise.

By doing this exercise you will develop your originality and ingenuity, and with them you will gradually awaken the courage of your individual approach to all that you do on the stage. As a result, you will later on be able to improvise on the stage quite freely at all times. This means that you will always find new, individual ways to fulfill old business, remaining within the frame given by the director. You will discover gradually that the real beauty of our art, if based on the activity of the Creative Individuality, is constant improvisation.

DISCERNMENT OF GOOD AND EVIL

Now for the second function of our Higher Ego. Everything in our art is built on the dynamic of the constant conflict between good and evil. This may seem to be an obvious truth, but consider how often we see artists—as well as people in everyday life—who are inclined to worship power as such, and to become intoxicated by it without distinguishing what kind of power it is. It is well known that this acceptance of unqualified and limitless control over others is detrimental to our social order.

It is not so obvious to the actor in his own sphere, however, that the inability to distinguish between good and evil makes his character flat on the stage. He misses all the various nuances in his performance and forces himself to bluntly express the notion of power in general. All sorts of clichés, bodily tensions, and so on, creep into the actor's work. He loses the aim of the author, which is always hidden behind the fight between good and evil in whatever form it may appear. He kills the ethical aspect of the play. He makes himself, the author, and the performance foreign to the present time, in which good and evil, right and wrong, are burning problems and driving factors. He enfeebles the sense of truth in contemporary society. On the other hand, good and evil, if they find response and comprehension, can give the actor the key to the very heart, the dynamic and inner composition, of the play and of acting itself. The ability to distinguish between good and evil is also the function of our Higher Ego. This ability can be increased by means of exercises.

EXERCISE 13.

Again appeal to your Creative Imagination, but this time your task will be to find out what particular kind of positive or negative impulses are conflicting in a play. What kind of evil is represented in King Claudius, Cornwall, Edmund, Iago, Polonius, Richard III? What and how positive are the characters opposing them? In what way is this opposition expressed? What possibilities for positive qualities lie in King Claudius, Caliban, and Rosencrantz? Wherein lies the charm of Edmund, Iago, Malvolio, Falstaff, Queen Anne, and Gertrude?

Not only will innumerable nuances become clear to you through such practice, but you will also see the meaning of artistic disguise, when evil hides behind the mask of good and good glimmers through the mask of evil. You will see that there never can be unqualified good and evil on the stage. By the same token, there cannot be undifferentiated power. Each manifestation of power speaks about a definite form of good and evil, the variety and interplay of which is unlimited.

CONTEMPORARY LIFE

Now let us speak about the third function of our Higher Ego. Since life, especially our contemporary life, is the manifestation of an enormous war between good and evil, expressed in countless variations, the actor must ask himself how he can relate his art to this panorama of struggle. It is through the medium of the spectator that we find a full creative approach that links us to the world and its times.

Vakhtangov was asked how his suggestions as a director were embodied in the play in a manner that was inevitably "conveyed" to the audience. His answer was "I never direct before an empty audience room. From the first rehearsal, I imagine the theatre filled with the audience. When giving my suggestions or demonstrating to the actor this or that passage, I 'hear' and 'see' clearly the reaction of the imaginary audience and reckon with it. Very often I quarrel with the imaginary audience and insist upon my point of view." Vakhtangov knew only too well that people often want to experience something other than that which they need to experience.

A contrasting example is found in a well-known playwright who was reading his new play to a group of friends. He started reading with calm assurance, clearly and expressively. Soon he came to a highly dramatic incident; his voice trembled, but he overcame it and went on. Soon, however, he was forced to pause and drink a glass of water, and long before his listeners understood wherein the real drama lay, they heard sobs from the author and tears poured down his cheeks. At the end he was openly and sincerely crying, but completely swallowing the text at the same time.

The comparison is clear. Vakhtangov created for the audience, the playwright for himself. No doubt his drama was deeply moving, but it did not come through because he wrote it without any connection with an audience. Vakhtangov grew and developed because he was in contact with his contemporaries. His profession became for him a part of the social life of his time, and the audience became for him the transmitter of public opinion. He listened to it and kept pace with his time, but was never subservient to it. "Success" was never for him the measurement of audience approval nor journalistic immediacy, as is so often the case.

Vakhtangov was a rabid newspaper reader, but he was not looking for sensational themes that would satisfy the hungry spectator. Instead, current and contemporary reportage was consciously combined in his mind with scenes and characters from plays. As he read his newspapers, flashes of remote events in Shakespeare's tragedies and comedies, as well as sequences from modern plays, arose in his imagination. When he read plays he perceived through them the incidents of life itself. Both appeared before him in a new light. From the newspaper in his hand, he knew how he would produce or act *Richard III, Hamlet,* or *King Lear* in terms of the events of his time. All of this was because he was a strong individual, who comprehended the problem of good and evil, and knew how to open his consciousness to the audience and to humanity in general.

EXERCISE 14.

Concentrate on the plays, but this time you must add to your exercise an imaginary audience. You must see the theatre filled with the audience, an audience of today, which comes from the whirl of life, from its offices, its newspapers, radios, from private life, from its colleges, factories, political affairs, and so on. Before this imaginary audience you must act or direct your plays, and ask certain definite questions: What is the purpose of this play in our present time? What will the audience derive from it? What use will it serve in modern society? What feelings, thoughts, and will-impulses will it arouse in a contemporary spectator? Will it drug the audience and make it indifferent to the events of contemporary life with all its conflicts, or will it arouse in the audience a protest against negative powers? Does it amuse the audience by inflaming its lower feelings, or does it call upon its sense of humor and refresh it with sound laughter, as do Shakespeare's comedies? Which aspect of the play and characters must be stressed in the production of the play, and which should be made less significant in order to achieve a positive result for a contemporary audience? How will the audience leave the theatre after the performance? Will it be provoked by the performance to act in the world?

The modern director and actor must know the audience, its power and weakness, its leading and misleading influences. It cannot be dependent upon the second-hand opinions of "specialists," but must be based upon the personal experience of meeting the audience in imagination and in reality. Only then will the director or actor hear the powerful voice of public opinion and be able to struggle with it if necessary. To the extent that he has awakened his own higher self, he will feel himself tuned to the pulse of his times.

THE OBJECTIVITY OF HUMOR

The more conscientiously we develop our Higher Ego, the more this grants us the faculty of humor. When we can detach our immediate egotistical reactions from everyday emotional events and interactions, they often reveal themselves in a really humorous light. The more our higher self is trained, the more likely we are to leave personal things behind us. We become objective in our perceptions as the artist should. Many things that previously excited us emotionally, and therefore hid from us their humorous features, now show themselves completely. The Higher Ego frees humor in us by freeing us from ourselves. Of course, not all laughter comes from the developed self, and not all giggling is laughter.

An illustration of this point: Anton Chekhov was able totally to forget his self-interest in normal surroundings. His care for others often overstepped even the limits of reason. He allowed himself, for instance, to be tortured for hours by visitors whose only aim was to enjoy the presence of a famous man. His humor was as great as his capacity for self-denial; therefore, he saw more than the people around him, and often his quiet, unexpected laughter brought embarrassment to others because humor through self-denial was not known to them. Such a man laughs easily even at himself, at times when other people become irritated and angry.

Once, not long before his death, Chekhov was walking along the streets of Yalta. Suddenly a crowd of boys began to pursue him and heartlessly shout after him, "Old Anton Chekhov's got consumption! Old Anton Chekhov's got consumption!" They were provoked by his hollow figure with stooped shoulders and sunken, yellow cheeks. What was Chekhov's reaction? A warm smile lingered on his lips. Of course it was not broad humor; it was the quality of self-denial that gave him the ability to describe children with love and great humor.

Many years ago, in the depths of Russia, a hermit was living his last days. He was the last of the true religious mystics. He had spent forty years in religious exercises and had attained great spiritual heights. I had the happy opportunity of visiting him, and never have I met even in ordinary social life a gayer person or one who was able to laugh so heartily, easily, and fully! His small, bent figure, his old blue eyes, radiated contagious humor, which arose purely from his Higher Ego.

In this chapter we have discussed the four main functions

of the actor's Higher Ego. First, individual interpretation of the plays and parts; second, the ability to distinguish between the powers of good and evil; third, the relationship of the actor to the time in which he lives; and last, the objectivity of humor through the liberation of the actor from his narrow, selfish ego. All this widens the mental outlook of the actor, sharpens his perceptions, and makes his artistic work more significant.

3

OBJECTIVE
ATMOSPHERE AND
INDIVIDUAL
FEELINGS

OBJECTIVE ATMOSPHERE

Actors have differing conceptions about theatrical space. Some performers regard the stage as an empty space, occasionally crowded with sets, properties, and people, only to become vacant at other times of the day. For them, everything in the theatre must be visible and audible. Other actors know that this is not so. The stage is always filled with Atmospheres, the source of ineffable moods and waves of feeling that emanate from one's surroundings. The theatre, the concert hall, the circus, each has a specific and forceful Atmosphere that is peculiar to it. And often it is one of these special Atmospheres alone, independent of content or human talent,

26

that attracts spectators to the entertainment.

Read the biographies of great actors and you will see that, for them, even the severely limited size of the stage was a whole world, enveloped with magical Atmospheres, from which they could not clearly separate themselves. After a performance, some actors spent the night in their dressing rooms or in the wings of the stage, absorbing the intoxicating Atmosphere. These gifted performers were impelled to reexperience the interplay of Atmospheres that embraced them when they acted. The Atmospheres brought about a sense of exhilaration that strengthened their acting.

Actors who outgrow the phlegmatic conception of the stage as an empty space know that Atmosphere is one of their strongest means of expression, as well as an unbreakable link between them and their audiences. These artists always look instinctively for the Atmospheres around them in their everyday surroundings, and they find them everywhere. Each landscape, town, street, building, room, library hall, hospital, cathedral nave, crowded restaurant, hotel lobby with its bright confusion, small house, tension-filled operating room, secluded lighthouse, corridor in a locked museum, engine room of an ocean liner, deserted farm—each of these contains its own particular Atmosphere. The seasons of the year, the hours of the day, and the fluctuation of the weather speak to us of different Atmospheres. But we must open ourselves up to experience them.

The life through which we move is rich with this interplay of Atmospheres. The actor must apprehend all those Atmospheres with which he has come in contact. Atmospheres for the artist are comparable to the different keys in music. They are a concrete means of expression. The performer must listen to them just as he listens to music.

ATMOSPHERE AND CONTENT

Atmospheres enable the actor to create the element of the play and the part that cannot be expressed otherwise. For example, imagine Romeo speaking his words of love to Juliet without the Atmosphere of love. Although the spectator may understand the sublime text and enjoy the beauty of Shakespeare's verse, he or she will still miss something of the content. And what is this content? It is love itself. All feelings require a specific Atmosphere to be conveyed to the audience. Without these proper Atmospheres radiating from the actor, Shakespeare's words of love, hate, despair, and hope reverberate meaninglessly in empty psychological space. Atmosphere reveals the content of the performance.

THE BOND BETWEEN ACTOR AND AUDIENCE

Think of how many difficulties actors experience in establishing communication with their audience. Consider how many shallow means they employ in an effort to "trick" the audience's attention. The performance is in reality a mutual creation of actors and audience, and the Atmosphere is an irresistible bond between actor and audience, a medium with which the audience can inspire the actors by sending them waves of confidence, understanding, and love. They will respond thus if they are not compelled to look into empty psychological space.

ATMOSPHERE INSPIRES THE ACTOR

The actor will also receive the necessary inspiration for his acting from the Atmosphere directly. Just as in everyday life one speaks, moves, and acts differently when surrounded by different Atmospheres, so on the stage the actor will realize that the Atmosphere urges him to new nuances in his speech, movements, actions, and feelings. Undoubtedly he will enjoy the unbreakable series of improvised and unconscious details in his acting. He will not need to resort to clichés, nor will he fix his acting in a rigid way.

The space, the air around the actor, will always be filled with life, and this life—which is the Atmosphere—will also keep him alive as long as he maintains contact with it. Even a simple imaginary experiment will convince us of all this.

EXERCISE 15.

Let us say that you are reading the scene from *Hamlet* in which Horatio, the soldiers, and Hamlet himself are waiting on the terrace of Elsinore castle for the appearance of the Ghost of the dead king. Now imagine this scene, or a section of it, with the Atmosphere of tense foreboding expectation of an ominous appearance, apprehension, and gloom. Follow each gesture, each intonation of the voices, each movement of the characters. Be sure that they really are in harmony with the chosen Atmosphere. Do it several times until you are satisfied with your little imaginary "performance." Then change the Atmosphere a little—for instance, to tense expectation, foreboding of an ominous appearance, but now active, fiery, vigorous. Act the same scene again in your imagination and see what changes will occur before your mind's eye, in the voices, movements, actions, mise-en-scène, and other means of expression for the characters. Do it several times.

Compare the second scene with your first "performance" and then make another change in the Atmosphere. For instance, fill it with admiration for the unknown Ghost, see it as stately, solemn, quiet, reserved. Observe the characters again in their imaginary acting, compare this with the two previous "performances," make another change in the same Atmosphere, and so on. In doing so, try not to hurry with the results. Let the characters develop their own reactions to the subtle nuances that you make in the Atmosphere. This will "inspire" your imaginary characters. Suddenly you will realize that these images truly have an independent life.

The same kind of work that we have just done in our imagination can be done by the actor in reality while preparing a part. This is another means of rehearsing through which the actor will always discover new content, new meaning, new values in his part, new significant facets of the character, and new means of expression. It will bring his character into full harmony with the rest of the play and with other characters.

The director can organize the rehearsal period of a production so that different Atmospheres within a play will be investigated, decided upon, and rehearsed as exactly as the dialogue or mise-en-scène. The script can be marked with a succession of Atmospheres. The division of the play into scenes and acts need have no connection with the division of Atmospheres. These can be freely distributed to cover several speeches or an entire scene, or only a part of it, according to the interpretation of the play. As a result, the actor, instead of waiting for the inspiration of an Atmosphere to "accidentally come to him," will have before him a score of Atmospheres that he can consciously assimilate, rehearse, and perform.

The true function of the Atmosphere starts even before rehearsals have begun. The actor whose training has given him a sharp sensitivity toward Atmospheres will undoubtedly notice that his first and general acquaintance with the part fills him with a certain definite, all-embracing Atmosphere. This experience anticipates his future creation.

Actors, like other artists, experience an overwhelming sense of joy that precedes the beginning of new work. Frequently when a writer starts a project he may not have any definite plot or details, but simply a desire to create out of a certain Atmosphere: tragic, humorous, dramatic, melodramatic, mystical, and so forth. This general Atmosphere, this "musical key," inspires him during the initial stage of his work. Characters, details, situations, and often, as we have said, the plot itself gradually occur before his mind's eye while he lives in this Atmosphere. But although we know about this process, rarely do we pay enough attention to it. When we fail to use Atmospheres consciously, an initial and important grip on our part is lost. Atmospheres at the beginning of an artistic endeavor are like a seed that contains the potential of the whole mature plant.

ATMOSPHERE STIRS PERSONAL FEELINGS

The Atmosphere, like the well-developed imagination, stirs and awakens Feelings within us that are the essence of our art. One cannot live in the Atmosphere of the scene or the whole play without immediately reacting to it with one's Feelings. The Feelings, in this case, arise organically of themselves, without being forced or squeezed out of our soul.

Although the Atmosphere is akin to our personal Feelings and individual moods, it nevertheless differs from them greatly. Imagine, for instance, a group of people, each with his own mood, entering an old castle where every stone, cornice, staircase, doorway, every room and tower breathes the Atmosphere of unspeakable charm and the mystery of a lost age. It is there objectively in the air, created by no one, dependent on no one, yet strong enough to fight even the personal mood of the person who enters into its influence.

Let us take another example: a catastrophe on a crowded street. How many different personal moods are there? One person is afraid, another full of compassion, the third burns with a desire to help, a fourth is indifferent, but the objective Atmosphere of the horror of the catastrophe prevails over all the people concerned, regardless of their personal moods.

An important characteristic distinguishes the Atmosphere from individual Feelings. This is its objective existence outside of the individual. If we usually speak of personal Feelings as coming from within the individual and radiating themselves into his surroundings, so in speaking of an Atmosphere we have to imagine this process reversed; the objective feelings of an Atmosphere are coming from outside and are radiating themselves into the individual realm of Feelings.

Although both individual and objective Feelings may be different (and even belong to different realms—one comes from within, the other from without), often both are present at the same time and in the same "space." That is what our experience shows us in innumerable instances in life as well as on the stage. For instance, you may enter a room in which a gay, festive Atmosphere will envelop you, but your personal mood may be gloomy and depressed.

Now let us go on to some exercises for acquiring the technique of mastering the objective Atmosphere.

EXERCISE 16.

Imagine the air around you, or a theatre space, filled with the Atmosphere that you have chosen. It is no more difficult than imagining the air filled with light, dust, fragrance, smoke, mist, and so on. You must not ask yourself, "How can the air be filled with fear or joy, tenderness or horror?" You must try it practically. Your first effort will show immediately how simple it is. What you have to learn is how to sustain the imaginary Atmosphere that now envelops you. Your main aid will be a developed Concentration (as discussed in Chapter 1). In this exercise you do not need to imagine any special circumstances or events to justify the Atmosphere. It will only distract your attention and make the exercise unnecessarily complicated. Do it as simply as described above.

After a certain period of time, when you feel sure of being able to imagine and sustain the Atmosphere around you, proceed to the next step. Try to relate the reaction inside you to that of the imaginary Atmosphere outside. Do not force yourself to feel anything, simply realize the reaction, which will appear of itself if the first part of this exercise has been carefully and patiently done. The whole value of this exercise will be lost if you impatiently impose the reaction upon yourself, instead of letting it grow freely. In the beginning this exercise may take time, but very soon you will see that the process of creating the Atmosphere and reacting to it is almost instantaneous. Gradually the Atmosphere will penetrate deeper and deeper into the realm of your emotions.

EXERCISE 17.

Now move and speak within the Atmosphere. Start with simple movements and a few words, trying to establish full harmony between them and the Atmosphere. Frequently, we are able to maintain a strong Atmosphere if we are silent and motionless, but as soon as we speak or make a movement we are inclined to destroy it. The Atmosphere must remain around you and your movements and words must be born out of it. The harmony will be achieved more easily and organically if you avoid any pretension, any attempts to "perform" such harmony as if someone were looking at you. Strive for the harmony sincerely and honestly, for the sake of the harmony itself, but not in order to "show off." Movements and words may gradually become more complicated. Finally you may choose short moments from actual plays and use them for your exercises.

Soon you will reach the point where your speech

and movements will intensify rather than diminish the Atmosphere. You can strengthen this result by making the effort to radiate the inner life that has been awakened in you through the objective Atmosphere.

To summarize:

1. Imagine the air around you filled with a certain Atmosphere.
2. Become aware of the reaction within you.
3. Move and speak in harmony with the Atmosphere.
4. Radiate it back into the space around you.

INNER DYNAMIC

The more an actor advances in acquiring the technique described above, the more he becomes aware of a certain peculiarity about Atmosphere. He begins to realize that it is never static, but dynamic, that it is a process rather than a state. It lives and moves constantly, although this movement is a purely inward, invisible, psychological one. If, for instance, the actor lives in a "depressing" Atmosphere, he definitely feels the pressure as an act, a process, or a movement that goes on unceasingly as long as the Atmosphere lasts. If the actor, through exercises, has really acquired a sense of inner dynamic, it will become for him an urging power, an impulse, an inspiration for his imagination and acting.

In Atmospheres such as catastrophe, panic, haste, excitement, gay festivity, etc., the inner movement, the urging power, is obvious. But what of Atmospheres such as the tranquillity of a forgotten cemetery, the comfort of a warm room, the peace of a summer evening? Here the inner dynamic is not so apparent. Yet for a sensitive actor, it exists in these apparently passive Atmospheres even as in those more energetic ones. The experienced performer knows and loves the catalytic power of the Atmosphere, which awakens his activity. He needs it on the stage if the theatre is to represent an expanded life for him and not merely a feeble reproduction of his usual surroundings.

The layman, the nonactor, surrounded by the Atmosphere of a moonlit summer evening, will remain impassive, while the actor, inspired by it, will start to act, at first perhaps in his imagination and then perhaps outwardly, too. Images born out of the inner dynamic of the Atmosphere will surround him. He will absorb this hidden dynamic and will transform it into events, characters, words, and movements.

MISSION OF ATMOSPHERE

Deprived of Atmosphere, a performance becomes greatly mechanized. It can be intellectually understood, its technical skill can be appreciated, and yet it will remain cold and heartless. This obvious fact is often obscured by the individual feelings of actors flashing here and there during the performance. But separate actors are only parts of the whole, and have to be united with each other and with the audience to create a performance that is an organic whole. How can they do this if they are not enveloped in one Atmosphere? The best way to create a chaotic performance is to cast a play exclusively with stars, and to let them display their brilliant abilities freely.

As we know, art itself lives primarily in the realm of feelings. The Atmosphere, which also belongs to this realm, is the heartbeat of every piece of art, and is also the lifeblood of each performance. In a materialistic era such as ours, people are ashamed of their feelings. They suppress and hide them. Are they not thus in danger of losing them altogether? The great mission of the contemporary actor is to save the objective Atmosphere in the theatre and with it to rescue the human facet of his profession.

INDIVIDUAL FEELINGS

Now let us consider the individual Feelings of the actor and ways to awaken them. It is possible for the imaginative actor to "see" the Feelings of his characters and the Atmospheres of the play. This enables him to become free of his conventional and personal responses, making his Feelings flexible and engulfing him in an infinite sea of surprising and varied nuances. Now the actor can receive the impulses for individual Feelings from outside.

But this does not exhaust the actor's possibilities of arousing and kindling his individual Feelings—the source of which lies within himself and is therefore most obscure. How often the actor tries to force his Feelings, to order himself to become sorrowful, gay, or happy, to hate, to love. It seems that such forcing is rarely successful. In most cases, the actor's Feelings, the most valuable element in his profession, remain dormant in spite of all his efforts. This is why he so often seeks refuge in his old theatrical habits and worn-out clichés. But since the actor's Feelings cannot be commanded, are there any other means of governing them at will? There are.

ACTION WITH QUALITIES

Let us try to describe a special technique for reviving the actor's Feelings. The secret lies in arousing the Feelings without forcing them immediately. If we want to lift and lower our arm, we are able to do it without difficulty. We can also do the same movement, let us say, cautiously. Of course, this will not seem any more difficult to us than our previous movement, but a certain psychological tint will come into our movement, namely, caution. How did this happen? It slipped into our movement, unnoticed by us as a Quality of caution.

But what is this Quality from the point of view of acting? It is nothing other than a feeling. Did we force it? No, it slipped into our movement just because we did not force ourselves to feel caution. We fulfilled our simple movement, our "business," and that we can always do. Our doing, our action, is always in our will, but not our Feelings. Here lies the key: the feeling was called forth, provoked, attracted indirectly by our "business," doing, action. If we had not acted but only waited for the appearance of the Feelings, perhaps they would not appear. On the other hand, if we only moved and acted, without coloring our action with Qualities, the Feelings might have remained passive.

We can go on doing different movements, choosing more complicated "business" with more complicated Qualities. We can, for instance, caress a child, speaking this or that word to it and giving our movements and voice the Qualities of warmth, tenderness, and compassion. Surely we will be able to do it just as easily as the previous simple tasks we set ourselves, but the difference in this case will undoubtedly be greater. The Feelings will take part in our acting to a great extent. We can combine a number of Qualities in our action, and in every case we will get the same result. We will have at our disposal Feelings—real Feelings—that will follow our movements, our actions, slipping into them easily and with sufficient strength.

Therefore, we can say that action with Qualities is the easiest way to the living Feelings. Once we have found the way to stir our Feelings without forcing them, we can be sure that they will flow of themselves more often and more easily. But this cannot happen without sufficient training.

EXERCISE 18.

Make simple movements and "business"—move your hands and arms in different directions, then get up or sit down, cross the room, take up different things, move them, and so forth. Make the same movement several times with different Qualities—calmly, fiercely, thoughtfully, angrily, hastily, staccato, legato, painfully, decidedly, slyly, wilfully, rigidly, softly, soothingly.

Go on doing this simple exercise until the Feelings begin to respond to the chosen Qualities. Then combine your movement and "business" with one or several words. The chosen Qualities must color equally both business and speech. If you are working with partners, proceed to simple improvisations. Later on even short sketches can be used.

The realm of Qualities is unlimited. You can take almost any noun or abstract idea, any image in your mind, and turn it into a Quality for your action. Try it practically and you will see how greedily the actor's nature turns everything into feelings if you approach the problem through the right channels.

ACTION IS "WHAT"; QUALITY IS "HOW"

Until now we have been speaking about Qualities that awaken Feelings when combined with Actions. But what about Action itself? Since the Quality is connected with the Feelings, so the Action comes from the realm of the Will. The Action, the movement, the gesture—what do they express? What do they speak about? They tell us what one's Will is aiming at.

Just like us in our everyday life, the characters on the stage always desire something. That means that the Will is always directed toward a certain goal, a certain aim. Out of this stirred Will, all Action, all "business," every gesture emerges on the stage, just as in life. The sharp, clear, definite aim of the Will expresses itself in well-formed, plasticly molded Actions and Gestures. While observing such Actions and Gestures we can penetrate into the Will of the character and follow its impulses and aims.

Now if we ask ourselves what the difference is between Action and Qualities, what each is assigned when combined together, we may say: the Action (and Will) expresses "what" happens, whereas the Quality (and Feelings) shows "how" it happens.

Each gesture, each Action, one makes, springs from a certain Will-impulse. The opposite is also true: the Gesture the actor makes can stir his Will. We have said that the more definite the Will-impulse, the more expressive the Gesture. Now we can add that the better the Gesture is formed, the stronger and clearer it is, the surer it will reach the Will and stir, stimulate, and arouse it. A strong Gesture of affirmation or denial, expansion or contraction, repulsion or attraction, will inevitably agitate the Will, calling forth in it a corresponding desire, aim, wish. In other words, the Will echoes the Gesture, reacts on it.

We must emphatically point out, however, that only Gestures that are properly done can arouse the actor's Will. He has to learn and practice making such Gestures in order to be able to apply them later on to the professional work. Therefore, let us first describe some exercises that lead to the correct technique for producing these Gestures.

EXERCISE 19.

Start with simple observations. Look at, or imagine, forms of different plants and flowers. Ask yourself, "What Gestures do these forms conjure before me?" Combine them also with Qualities. For instance, a cypress streams upward (Gesture), and has a quiet, positive, concentrated character (Quality); whereas, the old, many-branched oak, rising upward and sideways (Gesture), will speak to us of a violent, uncontrolled, broad character (Quality). The violet peeps out of its surrounding leaves (Gesture), tenderly, confidently, questioningly (Quality); whereas, the tiger lily thrusts out of the earth (Gesture), aggressively, persistently, passionately, almost shouting at us (Quality). Each leaf, stone, rock, remote mountain range, cloud, brook, wave, will speak to us about Gestures and Qualities that are contained in them.

Through such observations alone, you will awaken in yourself a living feeling also for each element of stage construction. You will, for instance, see different Gestures, the interplay of powers, and Qualities in staircases (steep or sloping), in doors, in windows (narrow, low, high, broad, or square), in pillars, walls, corners, etc.

It is amazing to see how Leonardo da Vinci experienced architectural form. "An arch," he says, "is nothing other than a strength caused by two weaknesses; for the arch . . . is made up in two segments of a circle and each of these segments, being in itself very weak, desires to fall, and as the one withstands the downfall of the other, the two weaknesses are converted into a single strength."

Would it not be true to say that Leonardo da Vinci "acts" the arch because in his imagination he is "inside" it? While exercising, you must try to do the same "acting," being inside the forms you are observing. Then try to make with your hands and arms the gesture that will express for you what you have experienced as Gestures and Qualities in different forms. Make this Gesture several times until you come to the point where your Will and Feelings will echo your Gesture.

Here, as in all exercises, you must make a real effort, but the final results should not be forced. These will come of themselves, if you are patient and persistent in your work.

EXERCISE 20.

Train yourself to make certain Gestures with the utmost expressiveness, as fully and completely as you can. These gestures might express, for instance: drawing, pulling, pressing, lifting, throwing, crumpling, coaxing, separating, tearing, penetrating, touching, brushing away, opening, closing, breaking, taking, giving, supporting, holding back, scratching. You can produce each of these gestures with different qualities: violently, quietly, surely, carefully, staccato, legato, tenderly, lovingly, coldly, angrily, cowardly, superficially, painfully, joyfully, thoughtfully, energetically.

The suggested movements must not become a kind of acting. You must avoid pretending, for instance, that you are pulling something with difficulty, and you are becoming tired. Try to adjust yourself to handle the imaginary heavy object more skillfully. Your movements of pulling, pressing, tearing, and others, must maintain a pure, ideal, archetypal form. Unnecessary complications and acting additions will weaken the results of this exercise.

Each movement must be as broad as possible, so that your whole body and the space around you will be used to the fullest degree. The tempo in which you produce your movements must be moderate, and after each movement come to the repetition of it without haste. Finally, the exercise must be done with full, inner activity, and yet you must not strain your muscles and body as you produce properly wide, broad but beautifully executed movements.

Through these exercises you will revive your body so that, later on, while producing smaller Gestures you will always feel as though your whole body—your whole being—takes part in them, although your whole body need not necessarily move. This is the point of the exercises. Your Will will not react to the movements if they do not occupy and electrify your body.

Another benefit of this exercise is the development of the ability to manage your body more freely than before. You will also more easily invent various Gestures and movements that you will need while applying "Action with Qualities" in your professional work.

EXERCISE 21.

Perform the Gestures with their Qualities again—the ones you found while working on the forms of different plants, flowers, and so forth. Perhaps you will improve them now, making them simpler but stronger and more expressive. Do each of them as many times as necessary to call forth the reaction of your Will and Feelings. Then go on doing them, but only in your imagination, remaining outwardly immobile. See that your Will and Feelings react upon the imaginary Gesture as they reacted upon the real one. If the result is not yet satisfactory, return to the previous stage and make your movements visible again, alternating them with invisible ones, and wait patiently for the result. If you do these exercises every day with the same energy, the result will show itself very soon.

Until now we have tried to describe how, by means of Gestures and Qualities, the actor can stir and awaken his Will and Feelings. Now as we continue we will see how he can apply these means to his professional work.

4

THE
ACTOR'S
BODY

*The body of an actor can be
either his best friend, or
his worst enemy.*
MARCUS AURELIUS

PHYSICAL-PSYCHOLOGICAL EXERCISES

There are no purely physical exercises in our method. These
would be useless, since our primary aim is to penetrate all of
the parts of the body with fine psychological vibrations. This
process makes the physical body more and more sensitive in
its ability to receive our inner impulses and to convey them
expressively to the audience from the stage. Our bodily exercises, therefore, are at the same time psychological ones, and
the actor who wishes to get the right results from the suggested exercises must remember this while working on them.

IMAGINARY CENTER IN THE CHEST

EXERCISE 22.

Imagine a Center in your chest from which living impulses are sent out into your arms, hands, legs, and feet. Start to move, imagining that the impulse to form the movement comes from this Center. Feel the aesthetic satisfaction that arises in your body. Remember not to move your arms from the shoulders and elbows or your legs from your hips and knees. Let the impulse of the movements from the Center in your chest break through these points where they may have been arrested before. The movements in the beginning must be simple ones, for example, raising and lowering the arms, taking a few steps forward and backward, sitting and rising.

Now try to realize that your arms and legs themselves start in the center of your chest. Walk through the room. The "Center" will lead you forward so the body cannot drag itself along. In the same manner move to the right, to the left, and backward. Gradually you will find yourself more powerful and harmonious. Thus you will learn to appreciate your body anew.

Complete some simple business, such as moving some objects, cleaning the room, or packing a suitcase. Keep your attention focused on the Center until you become accustomed to it and get its impulses without thinking of it. In addition, while moving on the stage ever so slightly—perhaps only your finger moves—you will feel intense streams of power coming from your chest to your finger.

MOLDING MOVEMENTS

EXERCISE 23.

Make abstract movements with your hands, arms, legs, and feet, and finally, with your whole body. Your task is to fulfill all these movements with inner power and awakened activity, so that you will feel as if you mold the air, or even a thicker, heavier substance, around your body. Each movement must leave an outline in your surroundings. Muscular tension is not necessary. The meaning lies in the psychological power of Molding, of overcoming the imaginary resistance and in giving the imaginary substance a definite form. The movements must be broad, full, and clearly differentiated from one another. Vague and indefinite movements have no place in this exercise. Do the movements in different tempos, with different intensities; even in slow and Molding movements, the power and awakened activity must not slip away from your consciousness.

Drop the idea of Molding the air around you. Complete any business, as was suggested, and let the Molding character in your movements live in you inwardly by itself, without your special attention to it. Create some simple improvisations.

FLOWING MOVEMENTS

EXERCISE 24.

The second kind of movement is a Flowing one, in which every movement is slurred into another in an unbroken line. Although they must be well shaped, these movements must have neither a beginning nor an end, but must flow into one another organically. Here it is also necessary to have activity and a certain power, but the character of the movement must be wavelike, growing and subsiding. Change the tempo. The element of air must be felt around you, as if it were the supporting surface of a wave. Use the same kind of simple movements as in previous exercises and then begin your improvisations.

FLYING MOVEMENTS

EXERCISE 25.

The third kind of movement we call Flying movements. While making these movements you must imagine that each of them continues in space indefinitely, flies away from you, departing from your physical body. Imagine also that your whole body has the tendency to lift itself from the ground. Such movements will arouse in you a desire to sustain them, as though to give them the time to fly away into space. Link one movement to the next continuously and freely, although not so slurred as in the Flowing exercise. Change the tempo. Your activity and inner power in this exercise will naturally take on a special character, but still they must be present to protect you from "sweetness" and sentimental enfeeblement. The element of air, in this exercise, must be experienced as one that stirs and urges. Start simple improvisations.

RADIATING MOVEMENTS

EXERCISE 26.

The last movement exercise has to do with Radiating movements. Imagine that invisible rays stream from your movements into space, in the direction of the movement itself. Send out these rays from your chest, arms and hands, from your whole body at once, in the direction in which you have moved. The desire to radiate will teach you gradually what kind of movements are more suitable for this aim. Some of them will take on a staccato character, some will be more legato, others will follow one after the other in unbroken succession. In this exercise you will try to radiate and send out the inner activity during your movements. Avoid mistaking physical tension for radiation. Change the tempo. Air filled with radiant light is the element of this exercise.

EXERCISE 27.

After you have assumed the specific characters of these movements, proceed to a simple improvisation or sketch. Each time, you and your partners must set yourselves a definite task. You must decide which kind of movement you will use in the improvisation. Then, whatever you do must be permeated with one of the four kinds of movement. Later in the improvisation, choose spontaneously the type of movement most suitable for the situation.

The result of such exercises will be that you will gradually feel yourself inwardly richer and outwardly freer. In all of these four kinds of movements, the "Center" in the chest must be experienced as an active part of the body.

Those acquainted with Rudolf Steiner's Eurythmy and his Speech-Formation will easily recognize in the four suggested movements four elements: earth, water, air, fire, which play such an important part in Steiner's method of artistic education. A thorough knowledge of these elements, as they were described and used by Rudolf Steiner, will give the actor invaluable help.

In addition to Molding, Flowing, Flying, and Radiating, the actor should adopt three more psychological Qualities in order to make his body more artistic, flexible, and expressive on the stage. All of those Qualities can be found expressed in great pieces of art.

FEELING OF EASE

The first Quality can be characterized as one of lightness and ease. Look, for instance, at such massive creations as Rodin's "The Thinker," Michelangelo's "Moses," late Gothic architecture, or any other creation of this standard. You will see that the weight has gone, as it were, from these creations, the material has been overcome, and they are permeated with ease and lightness, which also fills us and makes us lighter. We can even say that the "weight" of such great creations is different from our usual perception of it. This is one of the elements of the so-called "uplifting" impressions of great art. Undoubtedly the artist must have this ability to express things in a light and easy way, in his psychological and physical makeup. An actor needs this perhaps more than any other artist. His material is his own body, and in accordance with his profession he uses his body all the time.

EXERCISE 28.

Remember different moments in your life when you were in a heavy, gloomy, or light and gay mood. Compare them, and you will realize that heaviness or lightness lived in your limbs as well as in your psychology at that time. Concentrate on this quality of lightness and ease, which will be the first guide as you try to obtain a Feeling of Ease.

Stand still with your feet on the floor. Realize that you are in an upright position. Make clear to yourself two different attitudes that humans can have while standing on the ground, the first of which can be expressed as follows: "I am bound to the earth and my weight draws me down to it." The second attitude can be expressed in these words: "My upright position frees me from the earth on which I stand. My inner inclination is upward and not downward." Concentrate for a while on the second attitude of mind. Return to this simple exercise as often as you can.

Make different, simple movements, repeating them several times, trying to get them easier and lighter until you gradually awaken in yourself a complete Feeling of Ease. Do not confuse ease with weakness or passivity. Inner strength must be present even in the lightest of movements. Start with small movements, then proceed to a larger and wider expansion of them so that in the end you can run and jump around the room, filled with the Feeling of Ease.

Now choose any simple business and accompany it with a few words. Fulfill this task with the utmost inner and outer ease. You will learn, later on, to apply this quality on the stage, even when performing heavy movements, heavy moods, psychologically depressed moments, or when using heavy speech. The latter will lose its flat, blank character, it will not depress the audience, but will become art, even while expressing the heaviness required by the play. "Grace is ease in force," wrote John Ruskin.

This will prevent you from falling into banal photographic representation of so-called "real life," which can be taken only as a theme, and not as a manner of acting. When the Feeling of Ease becomes a permanent ability for you, you will use it unconsciously.

The Feeling of Ease is akin to the Flowing, Flying, and Radiating Movements. We can say that it even comprises all of them. The Feeling of Ease is the general basis on which all four of the actor's previous abilities can grow, develop, and unite themselves in his nature. The actor will be able to produce Molding Movements in a more correct and artistic way through the general Feeling of Ease.

The Feeling of Ease is also related to humor, a crucial aspect of art. The more hearty gaiety the actor brings into all his exercises the better. The Feeling of Ease can achieve this light tone. Humor cannot be squeezed out of the actor's nature any more than can any other human feelings. It must be simply welcomed when it is there and then it will be helpful.

FEELING OF FORM

Another outstanding quality that distinguishes all great pieces of art is clearly expressed in form. Even in their unfinished works the great masters always had a strong tendency to express a complete form. Their creations would have remained volcanic but chaotic if they had not imposed a strong form upon them. Only feeble, weak creative impulses fail to impart the necessity for form, perhaps because there is nothing there worthy of form.

The actor cannot deny form, for he must always deal with the form of his own body. The human hand is constructed in such a way that it is almost a crime to abandon it to vagueness. Look at the expressiveness of the fingers when they are put in different positions. The same is true of the arms and shoulders, the neck, the back, the legs and feet—the whole body. To give a strong and harmonious impression, our Feelings and Will-impulses must be equally well shaped on the stage, together with the movable forms of our body. Now let us see how the actor can develop a strong Feeling of Form so as to make it a part of his nature.

EXERCISE 29.

As the Feeling of Ease is akin to Flowing, Flying, and Radiating movements, so the Feeling of Form is akin to Molding movements. With this kind of movement you can start your exercises on form, but now you must pay attention to the following. First, whatever you do or say must have a clear beginning and a definite end. In this exercise you must not allow yourself to start or finish your movements, business, or words in a vague, sluggish way. This does not mean that you have to become rude and abrupt in everything you do or say on the stage. You can be very soft and mild in your expression but still have a very clear experience of the beginning and the end of what you are doing. Second, the more you exercise the more you must realize that really good form can be produced only from inside you. Emphasize this inner aspect of the form you produce, and see that these forms do not become outer, dead, empty shells. Third, before you start any of your simple movements or words, you must know what you are going to do and how you are going to do it.

EXERCISE 30.

Stand still and realize that your body is a form. Then "walk," in your imagination, with your attention focused within your body, as if molding it from inside, and also from outside. Realize that each limb of your body is a peculiarly built form. Then start to move your fingers, hands, arms, and so on slightly, realizing that your body is a movable form. This means that motion itself prevents you from being formless at any moment while you are moving.

In everyday experience we are entirely bereft of any Feeling of Form while moving our body. This must not be so for the actor if he wants to increase his expressiveness on the stage. After a certain period of cautious realization of his body as a movable form he will feel that his whole body is stronger, younger, and more obedient to the impulses coming from his inner life.

The next step forward is still more subtle and consists of assuming certain ideas concerning the body. These are extracted from Rudolf Steiner's teaching in the fields of art and Eurythmy. They are given here in a condensed form, for the actor's consideration.

Having thought over the threefold form of the human body, with its different general functions, the actor will gradually learn to appreciate and to use it in different ways. He will acquire a kind of "aesthetic consciousness" that will tell him how to use his body's various parts. An animal is bound to the earth with all four extremities, with its head bent toward the earth. The spinal column runs parallel to the surface of the earth. Man's position is upright, his head directed toward the universe. His arms and hands are free, his legs are bound to the ground but are freer than those of the animal. His head is connected with thoughts, ideas, and spiritual activity. In its round form it reflects the universe (macrocosm), becoming a kind of little world (microcosm). The head crowns the human body—it rests upon it.

The head is expressive only as a whole, through its different positions on the neck and shoulders; as a round form it cannot and should not make any "gesture"; that artificial smiling, forced frowning, imposed sorrow, and other "expressions" on the actor's face are nothing other than illegitimate attempts to make "gestures" with the head. The actor will become more and more adverse to the tendency to grimace, and will begin to prize the face as a "mirror" that freely radiates the actor's affections, moods, and so forth. The eyes will become especially expressive when the actor refuses to pull the fine muscles of his face forcibly, and real inner beauty will shine from such a free face.

The chest, arms, and hands are connected with the beating of the heart and rhythmical breathing. This is the sphere of the Feelings. The hands and arms are movable forms, permeated with feelings. As the freest of our organs, they are predestined for creative work, and are capable of expressing outwardly the inner life of man. How little we modern actors know about their expressiveness! Rhythm, which transforms and increases all the human feelings, making them into real material for art, is entirely neglected in our time. The fear of losing "naturalistic truthfulness" on the stage bars us from the real truthfulness of art. It will take a long time perhaps before we modern actors realize that naturalistic values will not suffer in the least from the fine, artistic "overtones" that envelop them in the form of rhythm. The arms and hands as movable forms, especially in connection with rhythm, have not yet been really discovered on the stage. When we hold our hands in our pockets or light one cigarette after another before the audience, we undoubtedly belittle the significance of our hands.

The Will dwells in the legs and feet. Their form expresses their function, which is to move the human body through space, according to man's ideas and feelings. See how characteristic and individual the legs and feet are when moving our bodies through space. The Will, such an impressive and expressive feature of the character on the stage, is often entirely forgotten by the actor while he is preparing a part. We sometimes get the impression, while watching a performance, that we see before us human beings deprived of Will. In any case, we often do not know what kind of will this or that character has on the stage. The legs and feet just do not take part in the acting. They pace back and forth without telling us anything about the character. But how rich and varied is the realm of the human Will!

Dr. Friedrich Rittelmeyer wrote: "There is a strong Will, which easily becomes lame, and there is a prolonged Will that grows on obstacles. There is a flexible, a stiff, a conscious Will, a sleepy Will, a contrary Will, which always wishes things different than they are, a social Will that works in one with great power when it feels that others share it, and an isolated Will, which loses its joy when others acquiesce with it. There is a straight Will, a crooked Will, an outer, an inner, non-spiritual, materialistic, an egotistical Will."*

I once saw an actor playing Othello. His performance as a whole was good, but what struck me most was his walk. Through it he revealed the whole mystery of Othello's Will to his audience! Each step of his Othello was an astonishing composition of a soft, gentle, loving Will; an inexorable, strong Will; a cautious, slow, penetrating Will; and at the same time an extremely passionate Will!

I was eager to know how he had acquired such a striking achievement and how he walked in ordinary life. He told me that, having found this walk at first in his imagination, he started to elaborate it. Later he acquired a special "eye" for studying the walks of different people that somehow resembled the walk of his Othello. Once he met a person on the street—I think it was in Italy—whose walk was just that of his Othello! The actor, unnoticed, started to pursue the person for weeks until he robbed him of his "Will"!

But what of this actor's everyday walk? Oh, it was most primitive and selfish! When he met a girl on the street his walk became humorously naive and betrayed his "Will" pitilessly! After having talked to him, I was attached to him more than ever before, because I understood that he must be a real artist if he could create such a miracle from his walk on the stage. Later on we became good friends. But the solution that this gifted actor found accidentally while working on his part, we can always put before us as a task when working on all our parts.

*Friedrich Rittelmeyer (1872–1938) was a biographer of Rudolf Steiner and a noted authority on Friedrich Nietzsche and German philosophy.

It would make a good exercise for the actor to observe the manner of walking of different people, trying to penetrate into the character of their Wills. Of course, the arms and hands are also filled with Will, but their activity is colored primarily by the Feelings.

What result can come to the actor from such meditative work upon his body as a threefold form? We realize that the body can be either "wise" or "stupid" on the stage. Neither evening dress nor Greek tunic can hide from the audience the impression the body makes from the stage. Have we not seen many times how the actor with a "stupid" body, speaking clever and even wise words from the stage, makes a pitiable impression, while the actor with a "wise" body, sometimes speaking insignificant words, still gives the impression that there is something significant going on on the stage. The actor's meditative efforts will, in time, make his body "wiser" on the stage.

FEELING OF BEAUTY

Everything has two sides, one that is right and the other, which is only a caricature of it. In human psychology, for example, if bravery is a virtue, senseless daring is not. If love is a true human feeling, sentimentality is its counterfeit. Caution is a useful quality, fear is destructive and useless. Likewise beauty, when it becomes a primitive "showing off," is an obvious caricature of itself, and is easily distinguished. But we are going to speak about genuine beauty, the finest quality the artist "lends" to his creation, if he has it within himself. Where are the roots of the right or wrong sense of Beauty? How can we distinguish them?

Let us look at manual laborers. We will see that their movements are often beautiful. When, for instance, the heavy hammer flies up and down again and again, the worker's mind is occupied exclusively with the task, without any desire to "show off." We may even say that true beauty must be hidden in order that others may discover it.

The Feeling of Beauty, which is deeply rooted in every artistic nature, should be found from within. It cannot be imposed from the outside because it is as individual as the artist himself.

EXERCISE 31.

Start with simple movements and "listen" attentively within you to the pleasure, the satisfaction, your limbs experience while moving. Move at first slowly, sifting away everything but the natural-born Feeling of Beauty. Avoid all weakness, sweetness, and sentimentality in your movement and do not neglect the inner strength. Do not go further in this exercise than is necessary to bring about the realization of this feeling within you. Let it grow of itself, as you continue the exercise. Resist the temptation to increase or stress the subtle vibrations of beauty. Let these vibrations radiate freely and "fill the air around with beauty," to quote Byron.

A noble satisfaction will arise in you if you are on the right track; not the satisfaction a person may experience when he wants to please someone who is looking at him. This noble satisfaction keeps all selfish elements beyond the threshold. Selfishness on the stage kills real beauty.

From simple and slow movements proceed to quicker and more complicated ones. Use words. Then try to make simple improvisations alone and with others. Finally, use some short sketches in the exercise. Repeat the work until you get the desired result.

Now the question may arise, how are we to perform characters and situations that are shocking and ugly in themselves?

For instance, how can we perform Caliban, or Richard III, or the scene from *King Lear* in which Gloucester's eyes are torn out? Will they become sweet, sentimental, and untrue if they are performed with a feeling of beauty? Of course not. The rudeness and ugliness must and will remain, but through the Feeling of Beauty on the part of the actor and the director, such scenes will be deprived of their realistic, inartistic rudeness, which appeals only to our lower, nervous, and physical reactions. They will be uplifted into a sphere that is higher than that of mere naturalism.

We shall always find a strong support for true beauty by breaking through the surface of the situation or character and by digging deeper into it. Intensive imagining is the means to this. The more superficially we consider a thing that is beautiful, the more sentimental it appears, while ugliness where taken superficially often calls up a feeling of disgust. For instance, the shocking rudeness of the scene in which Gloucester's eyes are torn out will immediately disappear if we consider the problem from a purely psychological aspect. If we do so, we will perceive that Gloucester loses his sight, his ability to perceive life, the faces of beloved persons, light, and colors. This psychological aspect must be stressed in this and later scenes, but not the physical aspect of it.

All these physical-psychological exercises make the actor's body more flexible and receptive to all inner impulses. But purely psychological exercises such as those on Concentration, Imagination, Atmosphere, and others also make his body more responsive, more sensitive.

5

THE
PSYCHOLOGICAL
GESTURE

*The soul desires to dwell with
the body because without the
members of that body it can
neither act nor feel.*
LEONARDO DA VINCI

PSYCHOLOGICAL STATES AND
GESTURES

All languages use idiomatic expressions related to physical
activity and gesture to describe complicated psychological
states. These imagined movements, which have become enchanted in our speech and thought, are gestures of everyday
life. But as applied to our psychological life, we produce them
in our minds instead of in our bodies. This is the only significant difference between the two kinds of gestures, since their
actual nature remains the same.

We "grasp" the idea just as we grasp the physical object.
We "touch" upon the problem just as we touch upon an

unknown surface in our physical surroundings. The spheres in which the gestures are produced are different, but not the gestures themselves. If the gestures were different, we would not be able to understand what it means to "touch upon a problem," for instance.

What does one do inwardly while uttering such expressions as these?

> To draw a conclusion
> To kill the thought
> To touch upon the problem
> To burst into tears
> To give comfort
> To break connections
> To grasp the idea
> To sidestep the responsibility
> To jump into the excitement
> To fall into despair
> To grow pensive

It would be a misunderstanding to conclude that we mean to imply that while we are "breaking" our connections with somebody, or are "drawing" a conclusion, we are actually producing "breaking" and "drawing" gestures in our mind as with our arms and hands. What we do mean is that the tendency to produce such a gesture undoubtedly exists in our mind. And this tendency is the same which stimulates us to produce physical "breaking," "drawing," or "grasping" gestures if such seem necessary.

Each individual psychological state is always a combination of thoughts (or Images), Feelings, and Will-impulses. We say that a human being or a character in a play "thinks," "feels," or "wishes" something because his thoughts, Feelings, or Will-impulses are the prevailing ones at that particular time. But all three functions are present and active in each psychological moment. Therefore, the psychological state in which the actor finds his character gives him the full opportunity to see it as the Action (or Gesture) with appropriate Qualities and Images. Thus, we may say that the same movement in one case is physical (Gesture) and in the other psychological (Qualities and Images). Let us coin for our future use the term "Psychological Gesture," which will mean the Gesture together with the Feelings connected with it. We shall apply this term to visible (actual) gestures as well as to invisible (potential) gestures.

PRACTICAL APPLICATIONS

Let's say the actor has a script before him. The author's excitement, imagination, feelings, creative ideas, his love, laughter, and tears are hidden behind the printed words. The actor's task is to unseal all these treasures, and there are two ways of doing it. One we may call the dry, intellectual approach, in which the plot, the content, the meaning of the words are understood, thought through. The consciousness skims over the surface of the Feelings, Atmospheres, and Images; aesthetic satisfaction is mentally achieved and the work is accomplished. The play is truly released—but not for the actor. To break the playwright's seal, he needs another means.

Aesthetic satisfaction alone will not help the actor. He is going to act, he is going to change, to transform his own Will, Feelings, and Imagination according to the play and to the characters in it. To achieve this aim, he must read the play several times, using his mind's eye more than his physical eye. He imagines the settings, the events, the characters; he listens to the words, to the voices; he sees the feelings of the characters, and inwardly follows their desires, lives in the interplay of Atmospheres, anticipates with excitement the reaction of his future audiences, desires the union with them, and so on. The play in the script begins to be a play in the actor.

The more he becomes acquainted with the play and the character, the more strongly his actor's intuition begins to raise its voice. Innumerable possibilities and individual ways are opened. The question is: Does the intuition flounder aimlessly, although happily, through the vast, motley world of awakened images, or is it led and directed by the actor himself? Here the guiding principle can be the Psychological Gesture.

With his sharp "gaze" the actor picks out here and there the Gestures—"what"—and the Qualities—"how"—which were discussed in Chapter 3. They arise before him, stirring his Will and Feelings. Some of them appear at once with the utmost clarity and urge him to produce them immediately, while others are not so easily grasped, but loom in the distance, promising, intriguing, stimulating. They accumulate, change, improve, influence one another. They merge in original compositions, flowing organically from each other, from the Atmospheres, from the situations, from the style, from the peculiarities of the characters.

When the actor is well trained and experienced in the technique of visualizing and producing Psychological Gestures, it is no longer a painstaking effort for him. He enjoys this kaleidoscopic, sparkling life of Images, Gestures, and Qualities. He has the right to enjoy it for a while, because it feeds his subconscious creative activity, and prepares him for the next period of more detailed work.

Even during this first period of joyful discovering of the Psychological Gestures, the actor will find that he has already acquired a fairly thorough knowledge about the whole play and his part. How did this happen? Did he analyze the play and the characters in a dry, intellectual way? Did he painstakingly compare the play with other dramatic creations in order to find their similarity, and then label the play and put it on the shelf? Did he search for the literary source of the play? Did he read the comments about it? No, he did none of these things—at least not yet!

The actor's approach was fresh, independent, direct, free, creative, and, most important of all, an actor's approach! What was the Psychological Gesture he used for his exploratory work? It was acting—inner participation in the life conjured behind the printed words of the author's script. His knowledge was not superficial. How could it be if through the Gesture he had experienced the Will and through the Qualities he had found the Feelings that the author himself had while creating his drama? He understands the plot, the content, no less than anyone else, but it is not centered in his brain only—it is spread over his whole actor's being. It lives in his hands, arms, torso, feet, legs, and in his voice. He feels capable of expressing it as an actor, but not as a critic or an analytical scientist. Through the Gesture with Qualities, he knows more true and profound things about the play and the character than the scientist ever could.

If knowledge through acting and for acting is the first achievement of the performer, then the second phase is a slow but sure process of adjustment and transformation of the inner life of the role. Through the experience the Psychological Gesture offers him, the actor enjoys the organic process of gradually "becoming" a character. From the very beginning of his study, he has been inside the character; his reward will be his own inner growth.

How much artistic satisfaction one can have by experiencing or even observing day after day how an actor transforms into a character! Even now I can vividly recall how this wonderful process could be clearly observed in its classical form, if I may say so, in Stanislavsky. As he studied his part, he grew more and more "a character." Unnoticeably to himself, he began to speak and to move slightly differently in his private life during this period of study. Although he never lost his childlike charm, he was nevertheless psychologically changed. And I must admit that if we who were often in his surroundings had some questions or business to discuss with him, we always chose the day when he was playing a "good" or "wise" character, to assure the success of our business.

Please don't think even for a moment that this great artist was in any way possessed by his character. Not at all! Stanislavsky simply enjoyed "flirting" with the character, even during his everyday life outside the rehearsal room. He cherished the character, explored it deeper and deeper, refining it and his own psychology. But he was above the character and completely free from "forgetting himself." I shall always remember Stanislavsky's eyes when I acted with him on the stage. Oh, those eyes! While acting himself he watched his partner with a strong director's look, sometimes accusing, sometimes encouraging. He was fully aware of what was going on around him while he was, to use his own expression, "playing with the part." A great artist such as he could not become blind while creating.

One may protest that Stanislavsky did not use the Psychological Gesture. Of course, he did not "use" it; he grew into his character intuitively, being driven by his own genius. (We must not forget also that Stanislavsky had his own system, too.) But we are not writing a book about "genius in general." We are trying to find the technique for those gifted actors who want to consciously develop their talents, who want to master their abilities and not flounder aimlessly, relying upon vague inspiration. Such individuals as Stanislavsky, for instance, must be watched and studied. Conclusions must be drawn from such studies and classified and shaped into a method that can then be used by anyone who wants to have a defined technique. In other words, anyone who wants to see the theatre grow and develop in the future. That is what we are trying to achieve in the pages of this book, as a small and humble contribution to the great knowledge of the theatre, which will come gradually with new generations.

Now let us return to our theme. In the following exercises, we shall try to take a further step in our understanding of what the Psychological Gesture is and also to explain how it can be used for acting primarily.

EXERCISE 32.

The aim of this exercise is twofold. First, we are to develop sufficient skill in extracting the Psychological Gesture from the Imagination. Second, we shall learn to distinguish between the preparatory Psychological Gesture and the gestures the actor might use while acting. (Always keep in mind that the Psychological Gesture has nothing to do with various gestures the actor might use on the stage while rehearsing or performing.)

Take any play, preferably one with which you are not completely familiar. Imagine it, as we have described before, without choosing any part for yourself. Continue imagining until the events and characters of the play become a living performance for you. While doing so, fix your attention on moments which for this or that reason seem significant or expressive to you. Concentrate on the character that appears central in the moment you have chosen. Ask this character to act before you in your Imagination and follow its acting in all details. Simultaneously, try to "see" *what* the character is aiming at, *what* is his wish, his desire? In doing so, attempt to avoid reasoning, but rather seek to penetrate as clearly and vividly as possible into the character's *what* by means of the image before your mind's eye. As soon as you begin to guess *what* the character is doing, try to find the most simple Psychological Gesture for it. Do it physically, looking at the same time at your image.

Improve the Psychological Gesture in its simplicity and expressiveness by exercising it. Do not ask your imaginative character to do the Psychological Gesture for you. It is useless. The character must only act in terms of the play. Hamlet, for instance, when the curtain is raised, can sit motionless in the throne room. This is your imagination. But Hamlet's Psychological Gesture might be a large, slow, heavy movement with both arms and hands, from above downward toward the earth. You may find this Gesture right for Hamlet's dark, depressed mood at this time of his life. And this Gesture is what you must do in reality, while you are watching your image.

Then try to act and to speak like Hamlet, having now the Psychological Gesture only in the back of your mind, as it were.

Do the Psychological Gesture and the acting alternately, until it becomes evident to you that behind each internal state or movement in acting is hidden a simple and expressive Psychological Gesture that is the essence of the acting. King Claudius, watching the performance of *The Mousetrap* play, may have as the inner Psychological Gesture a long, excruciating gesture of falling backward with raised arms and hands and widely spread fingers, while his actual stage acting can be very economical in movement and even opposite to the Psychological Gesture—for instance, it may be a slow contraction of the whole body. Boastful Falstaff may have big, brave, unbridled acting gestures, while the invisible Psychological Gesture that inspires the actor can be a small, cowardly, compressing one—as if he holds in his hand a small piece of paper that he crumples.

Take other moments from your imaginary performance, studying them in the same way. The Psychological Gesture will appear before your mind's eye and, after being practiced, will always remain with you as a kind of inspiration while you are acting. While exercising the Psychological Gestures you may use Qualities as well, which will make your exercises more pleasant and beneficial.

EXERCISE 33.

While working on his part, the actor may find it necessary to apply the technique of Psychological Gesture, especially to the text. Let us see how this can be done. As an example we will take the following lines of Horatio (*Hamlet*, Act I, Scene I).

(Reenter Ghost.)

HORATIO: I'll cross it, though it blast me.
           Stay, illusion!
           If thou hast any sound, or use of voice,
           Speak to me:
           If there be any good thing to be done,
           That may to thee do ease, and grace to me,
           Speak to me:
           If thou art privy to thy country's fate,
           Which happily foreknowing may avoid,
           O! speak;
           Or if thou hast uphoarded in thy life
           Extorted treasure in the womb of earth,
           For which, they say, you spirits oft walk in death,
           Speak of it: stay and speak! Stop it, Marcellus.

The actor's imagination may conjure up Horatio in an extreme state of mental excitement that drives him through his whole speech. There are many variations and nuances in this short speech, but first the actor needs to find its main dynamic. He listens inwardly to Horatio's lines and intuitively seeks the possible Psychological Gesture that may be hidden behind them. The actor skips over the fine nuances in Horatio's speech; instead he looks for the characteristic Gesture. Let us assume that his Gesture is a sharp thrust forward with his body, his right arm and hand directed toward the Ghost. To fix the unknown being can be the desire, the "what," of the Gesture, while commanding excitement can be its Quality, the "how."

After the actor begins to practice this Psychological Gesture, the power and the character will appear while he is speaking the lines, making it colorful and strong. The danger of using the text only for its dry intellectual content, for its meaning only, becomes diminished. The "how," the artistic side of the speech, comes into the foreground. The plain meaning, the "what" of the word, will never be lost, since the actor understands what the author speaks about, but the "how" will suffer greatly if the actor does not build it on the basis of a dynamic Gesture with its demonstrative qualities. "If speech is to be made plastic on the one hand, musical on the other," wrote Rudolf Steiner, "then this is first of all a matter of bringing gesture into the speech."

The actor exercises the Gesture as long as is needed to stir his inner life. The Psychological Gesture becomes for him a kind of a first, rough, charcoal draft for the future picture, after which all the details will gradually emerge and cover the initial sketch.

Having completed this preparatory stage, the actor finds a few characteristic leading words in the speech and pronounces them while making the Psychological Gesture. In our example, he may distinguish among a chain of energetic exclamations, which are so typical for this particular speech:

I'll cross it, though it blast me.
Stay, illusion!
If thou hast any sound, or use of voice,
Speak to me:

If there be any good thing to be done,
That may to thee do ease, and grace to me,
Speak to me:
If thou art privy to thy country's fate,
Which happily foreknowing may avoid,
O! speak;
Or if thou hast uphoarded in thy life
Extorted treasure in the womb of earth,
For which, they say, you spirits oft walk in death,
Speak of it: stay and speak! Stop it,
Marcellus.

By doing so the actor's concern must be that the words sound more and more in harmony with the Gesture, that is, with its "what" and "how."

EXERCISE 34.

The best way to rehearse the words selected from Horatio's speech (or any other passage) would be the following: At first, execute the Gesture without words, then the Gesture with words together, and finally, only the words without the Gesture. The strength and all the qualities of the Gesture are thus poured into words and become audible.

EXERCISE 35.

The exclamations must receive their nuances. The image of Horatio reveals to the actor that his excitement can grow simultaneously with the failure of his intention. This can be the basis for finding the first nuances from the general Psychological Gesture. It can be transformed into seven different Gestures in accordance with the seven exclamations. If the first of them can be imagined as comparatively slow, sure,

DRAWING 1

Imagine that you are going to play a character which, according to your first general impression, has a *strong* and unbending *will*, is possessed by dominating, despotic *desires*, and is filled with *hatred* and *disgust*.

You look for a suitable over-all gesture which can express all this in the character, and perhaps after a few attempts you find it (see Drawing 1).

It is *strong* and well shaped. When repeated several times it will tend to strengthen your *will*. The direction of each limb, the final position of the whole body as well as the inclination of the head are such that they are bound to call up a *definite desire* for *dominating* and *despotic* conduct. The *qualities* which fill and permeate each muscle of the entire body, will provoke within you feelings of *hatred* and *disgust*. Thus, through the gesture, you penetrate and stimulate the depths of your own psychology.

DRAWING 2

This time you define the character as aggressive, perhaps even fanatical, with a rather fiery will. The character is completely opened to influences coming from "above," and is obsessed by the desire to receive and even to force "inspirations" from these influences. It is filled with mystical qualities but at the same time stands firmly on the ground and receives equally strong influences from the earthly world. Consequently, it is a character which is able to reconcile within itself influences both from above and below (see Drawing 2).

DRAWING 3

For the next example we will choose a character that in a way contrasts with the second. It is entirely introspective, with no desire to come in contact either with the world above or below, but not necessarily weak. Its desire to be isolated might be a very strong one. A brooding quality permeates its whole being. It might enjoy its loneliness (see Drawing 3).

Much, too, depends on the tempo in which you exercise the PG once you have found it. Everybody goes through life in different tempos. It depends mainly on the temperament and the destiny of a person. The same must be said for the characters in plays. The general tempo in which the character lives depends largely on *your interpretation* of it. Compare Drawings 2 and 3. Do you recognize and feel how much faster is the life tempo of the former?

DRAWING 4

For the following example, imagine a character entirely attached to an earthly kind of life. Its powerful and egotistical will is constantly drawn downward. All its passionate wishes and lusts are stamped with low and base qualities. It has no sympathy for anyone or anything. Mistrust, suspicion and blame fill its whole limited and introverted inner life. The character denies a straight and honest way of living, always choosing roundabout and crooked paths. It is a self-centered and at times an aggressive type of person (see Drawing 4).

DRAWING 5

Still another example. You might see the strength of this particular character in its protesting, negative will. Its main quality may seem to you to be suffering, perhaps with the nuance of anger or indignation. On the other hand, a certain weakness permeates its entire form (see Drawing 5).

DRAWING 6

This time your character is again a weak type, unable to protest and fight his way through life; highly sensitive, inclined to suffering and self-pity, with a strong desire to complaints (see Drawing 6).

Here also, as in the previous cases, by studying and exercising the gesture and its final position, you will experience its threefold influence upon your psychology.

DRAWING 7

Take as one more illustration the PG of *calmly closing your-self* (see Drawing 7). Find a sentence corresponding to it, perhaps: "I wish to be left alone." Rehearse both the gesture and the sentence simultaneously, so that qualities of restrained will and calmness penetrate your psychology and voice. Then start making *slight* alterations in the PG. If, let us say, the position of your head had been erect, incline it slightly down-ward and cast your glance in the same direction. What change did it effect in your psychology? Did you feel that to the quality of calmness was added a slight coloring of *insistence, stubbornness*?

and legato in its Quality, then the last one should be quick, uncertain, and staccato. The five Gestures in between build a transition from the first to the last one. The actor now rehearses these seven Gestures and, as described above, watches carefully that the words sound harmoniously with the new qualities of the new Gestures.

EXERCISE 36.

Still another suggestion comes from the Imagination: with awe toward the unknown being, Horatio starts his speech, while he ends it with offensive coarseness. Reason and dignity also decrease in his attitude. The "what," the intention—to fix the unknown apparition—remains the same, or even increases. The seven Psychological Gestures change in their Qualities. They acquire new nuances. The positions of the whole body, of the arm and hand, are commanding and animated as before, but now are filled with respect and held in reverence in the beginning, while at the end they lose more and more their honor, becoming aggressive, lacking in awe and even insulting. This change takes place organically from the first to the last of the seven gestures.

TRANSITIONS

In the same way the actor has found the seven characteristic Gestures throughout the whole speech, he can also find the Transitions between them. With new Psychological Gestures he can fill the gaps between the chosen words and animate parts of the text as yet untouched. Filling, for instance, the first gap, "If thou hast any sound, or use of voice," the actor may find that these words are filled with Qualities of hopefulness, adoration, and perhaps warmth. So after the first request, "Stay, illusion," he may make a broad, pleasantly full swinging movement with his right arm and hand and come to the point, "Speak to me," firmly concluding the first transition. This Gesture should be rehearsed in connection with words, as was suggested above.

Each subsequent Transition between previously selected exclamations will demonstrate to the actor that the metamorphosis leads Horatio from awe, assurance, and admiration to coarseness, despair, and aggressiveness. Growing suspicion and impatience are more and more manifested, in spite of Horatio's strength. The Psychological Gestures representing the Transitions are swinging forward with ever growing sharpness, taking the whole body with them. The actor again rehearses these Gestures and their Qualities with the text belonging to them.

The actor must compare these transitional Gestures with each other so that they can influence one another, thus becoming harmonious in composition. He finds all the transitions he needs in the form of Psychological Gestures, thus filling the spoken words with power, expressiveness, life, individual psychological nuances, rhythms, and so forth. But, just as before, he does not need to use all the words at once, especially in more complicated and longer passages. He may do well to follow the principle of selecting leading words throughout the whole speech that has been chosen for the work, and only gradually adding new words. Such means of using the text should guarantee that each word will be thoroughly animated. Later the actor will love such striking words, not for their meaning only, which will very soon leave him cold, but for their artistic value, which he himself has given them. Animated words have wings and surely will always reach the audience.

Above, in our example of Horatio's scene, we have spoken about Transitions the actor must find between the two chosen moments in the text. A peculiar ability of the actor's nature enables him to make any transitions between any chosen moments without any "logical" justification. All actors know in themselves this amazing ability, but not all of them use and develop it sufficiently. They have acquired a bad habit of jumping from one obvious moment in acting indicated by the author to the next without any Transition. It seems to be "logical" to the modern actor, but he often overlooks the fact that through such "logic" his acting becomes dry and primitive. True, the onlooker follows the development of the plot, but he is not interested in the acting itself. Quite the opposite happens when the actor uses his ability of making free transitions in his acting. His very individuality becomes visible through the network of his fine Transitions. His acting becomes rich and intriguing for the audience.

The talented actor reads the play. The nonactor, or spoiled actor, reads the same play. What is the difference between the two kinds of reading? The nonactor reads the play absolutely objectively. The events, happenings, and characters in the play do not stir his own inner life. He understands the plot and follows it as an observer, an outsider. The actor reads the play subjectively. He reads through the play and by doing so he inevitably enjoys his own reaction to the happenings of the play, his own Will, Feelings, and Images. The play and the plot are only a pretext for him to display, to experience the richness of his own talent, his own desire to act. The nonactor reads the lines while the actor reads between the lines, sees beyond the characters and events of the play. These magic "beyond" and "between" places make up that kingdom in which the talented actor lives and moves freely. From his kingdom he sees the whole play as a stimulus, as a series of signs and indications behind and beyond the words urging and guiding him in his individual acting. He enjoys his innumerable free transitions, linking the signs together.

But what are the indications and signs given by the author or director? What are the starting and final points the actor moves between, acting freely? Are there logical reasons for his acting and for his Transitions? Not at all! The reason, the only reason, is the inborn, natural ability to act! A sensitive actor will not be able to deny the fact that he can act without any plot, any play, any outer reason than just to act, perhaps for hours, going on and on, speaking, moving, passing through an unlimited flow of feelings, being overwhelmed by sorrow, joy, sadness, or happiness; being inspired to laugh and to cry, hoping, wishing, regretting, despising, forgiving, loving, burning, and cooling!

I remember Vakhtangov improvising scenes, characters, and events, starting without any "reason" or previously thought-out theme. He saw a pencil lying on the table; he picked it up. How he did it was for him the first link in an endless chain of improvised moments. The hand grasped the pencil somewhat clumsily, and immediately on his face and in his whole figure one could see a simple lad. Sitting down at the table he slowly drew with his pencil the letters of a girl's name. The lad was in love! Another face, another expression of the eyes. But before the name was fully written down, a big, round point concluded the writing. The lad's cheeks became pink. He was shy and tongue-tied. A bashful smile lingered on his lips. He got up and saw a mirror on the wall. The whole gamut of emotions shot through the soul of the lad in love: hope, doubt, longing, the desire to look handsome, still more handsome, still more. Tears moistened his eyes, the head came nearer and nearer to the glass and the lad in the mirror received a tender, hot kiss from the lad outside the mirror. He saw her, and only her alone.

So Vakhtangov went on and on, creating an unbroken chain of transitions full of unexpected little events. Often Vakhtangov set himself a definite task for his improvisations. For instance, he took an empty bottle and a match. His task was to improvise a drunken man who wanted to put the match through the neck of the bottle but was not able to do so. His inventiveness and his ability to improvise in such cases seemed to be inexhaustible.

The actor must learn to trust his own creative subconscious, and it can be done by persistent and patient exercising of the ability to make Transitions. Here is one such exercise!

EXERCISE 37.

Choose two simple contrasting psychological moments. For instance, one of them can be the word "yes," pronounced with wrath and power. The other can be the word "no," spoken softly and full of pleading. Pronounce this "yes," and then continue to act without any previously thought-out theme, knowing only that your final aim will be the pleading "no." Allow your soul to make a free and unbroken Transition from one pole to the other. Start with a very short Transition between "yes" and "no." Allow your soul to make a free and unbroken Transition from one pole to the other. Then, by repeating the exercise many times, try to extend the duration of the Transition as much as you can. While improvising such a transition, allow yourself to do and to speak whatever you like. Don't hesitate to grieve and to smile, to curse and to love, to implore and to command, to doubt and to believe. The more polarized your starting and final points are, the better. Then choose three (like cynicism to love to fear) and, later on, more points, and "travel" among them freely and, if possible, without any disturbing self-criticism. The ability to criticize oneself in the right way will develop gradually, and it should never be too conscious and too intellectual.

EXERCISE 38.

With a partner, invent your own starting and final points. Both of you should freely create your Transitions simultaneously. The new element in this case will be the need to deal with the improvised acting of the partner. The scene must run smoothly and harmoniously, as if it were already well-rehearsed. For this exercise, neither partner will need any "logical" justification while choosing their points. It can be "yes" and "no" for one of the partners, and "no" and "yes" for the other. It can be anything, any business, any word or any sentence, any starting or final position chosen at random. The less the points are "justified," the more pleasure from unexpected surprises will arise for both partners. Repeat the same Transition, allowing yourself to perform differently than you did before.

Proceeding in the direction discussed in the *Hamlet* example, the actor, appealing to his Imagination, will find more and more nuances in the seven Gestures after the general ground has been thoroughly prepared. The new experience should convince him that behind the spoken word is also an invisible movement. He will feel that the word is a Gesture that has been transformed into a sound. If it were not so, the spoken word would not have any power or any life in it. The hidden Gesture, "slipped" into the word, is the true driving force of the spoken word, and the actor needs it above all if he does not want to resemble orators whose words, hardly being uttered, fall down like dry, crisp leaves.

EURYTHMY

Not only the words but each sound of human speech can have a driving force. Speech Formation and Eurythmy, created by Rudolf Steiner, teach us first of all to distinguish between vowels and consonants as a means of artistic expression.*

*There are many useful books on Eurythmy. Among the best are: *Eurythmy and the Impulse of Dance*, Lundgren, Harwood and Raffe (Rudolf Steiner Press, London); *Eurythmy: Essays and Anecdotes*

The vowels are closely connected with our feelings and are more intimate for us than the consonants. The vowels, therefore, are naturally a more suitable means of expressing lyrical, spiritual themes and intimate experiences, whereas the consonants sound more dramatic, more heavy and earthy. They are, as it were, imitating the outer world, whereas the vowels express primarily the human feelings. The vowels are the music and painting of the human speech; the consonants are its plastic power.

Through practicing Eurythmy, the actor will become acquainted with a series of different Gestures connected with different vowels and consonants. Through them he will be able to animate each sound, in his artistic speech. Rudolf Steiner maintained that "Speech Formation must, for the speaker, of necessity be Art reaching to the point of sound, just as music must be Art reaching to the point of tone."

Let us take, for example, the sound of the letter "a" in "father." What Gesture lies behind it, creating it and giving it its power and audible content? Imagine that we open our arms widely and stand with our legs apart and follow with our feelings this Gesture, trying to experience it strongly. What do we experience? A kind of astonishment, awe, admiration, and similar feelings. What do we do while speaking the sound "ah"? We open our souls for questioning, admiration, and absorption of the impressions coming to us from within ourselves or from our surroundings in life. Even the vocal chords and mouth open, or have the tendency to open themselves widely while pronouncing the sound "ah."

While the feelings and the Gesture of the sound "ah" are that of awe, admiration, opening, expanding, and even going out of ourselves (in yawning, for instance, we tend to go out of ourselves to the extent of falling asleep)—quite opposite is the Gesture and the psychology of the sound "oo" (as in

(Schaumberg Publications, Roselle, Illinois); and *An Introduction to Eurythmy*, Rudolf Steiner (Anthroposophic Press, Hudson, NY).

"moon"). Here everything tends toward concentration, closing, and narrowing. Fear, cautious awakening, alertness is the
psychology of this sound. According to Rudolf Steiner, "To
feel small, stiffened, retracting, cold, that is what the 'oo'
sound awakens in the human soul."

The consonant sound "s" expressing the connection of the
human being to the outer world rather than the intimate
inner life of man has a calming power, which brings to
a poised state what was in movement. Through this sound
we penetrate deeply into the inner life of that which
is calmed by us. We can experience the nature of this
sound by doing the Eurythmy gesture of "s." We experience
its magical character by moving our arms and hands from
below upward in wavelike, winding, snakelike, sharp
movements in which one arm and hand follow the other with
little delay.

Eurythmy leads us thus through all the sounds of human
speech, through all the combinations of sounds, teaches us to
realize the mutual connection and interrelation of these
sounds, shows us endless variations of each of the sounds,
thus making our artistic speech into the finest possible mem-
brane of endless subtleties and variations of our psychology.

"Astonishment" and "awe," which become audible in the
"ah" sound, for instance, can be strong or mild, profound or
superficial, gloomy or light, serious or naive, stupid, humorous, sly, and so forth. And still it will always remain the same
"ah" sound with the same gesture and the same tendency of
"opening" behind it. We cannot invent new Eurythmical
gestures for the sounds of the human language, any more
than we can invent new "a" or new "b" or new "c" sounds.
They exist objectively. But we can vary and color them freely
according to our artistic impulses and tastes. The variety here
is as unlimited as in the Psychological Gesture, which we can
and must invent each time anew.

There will be many benefits for the actor who has exercised
his speech and animated each sound by means of Eurythmy.

First, harmony and natural beauty will permeate the speech and whole being of the actor and will lift him into the realm of art, where ugliness as a means of expression (not as a theme) ceases to exist. Second, the sound will become a fine transmitter of the actor's creative intentions. Third, sensitive feelings will be awakened in the actor's soul and will become accessible to him at his will. Fourth, the actor will learn to use speech as a means of characterization. Through his newly developed mastery to express in his speech the finest nuances of each sound of human language, he will be able to mold the manner of speech differently for each part he is going to act. The most subtle differences in pronunciation distinguish his characters one from the other. Bad is the author whose characters all express themselves with the same phrasing. Equally bad is the actor whose different roles on the stage always speak in the same unchangeable manner.

If there is any art of the theatre at all, it begins with acting and directing. The author and his play are not yet the theatre. Dramaturgy is independent of other arts; the theatre starts when the actors and the director take the written script into their hands. Their Creative Individualities are what make the theatre. The actor begins to explore the play, and as he does so, he must explore himself. All the lines, all the situations in the play are silent for the actor until he finds himself behind them, not as a reader with good artistic taste, but as an actor whose responsible task is to translate the author's language into the actor's. The written word must become the spoken one.

The search for himself, to find himself, is the reason why the actor must leave the beaten track. What does it mean for the actor to find himself? It means one thing: to find the contact with his own Creative Individuality. The Psychological Gesture and Eurythmy are the paths for the actor to fulfill this great task.

SENSITIVITY

To acquire full use of the Psychological Gesture, the actor must develop greater sensitivity to the nuances of his body. He can achieve this by doing certain exercises.

EXERCISE 39.

Choose any simple Psychological Gesture, but do not define its Quality. Also, choose a sentence to be pronounced with the Gesture. Let us suppose that you have chosen as a Gesture a wide movement of enclosing yourself with your arms, and the sentence "I want to be alone." Execute the Gesture and try to guess the Qualities that can be aroused by the Gesture itself. Now speak the sentence so that it sounds in harmony with the Gesture and its Qualities. Do this several times fully and completely, in order to become familiar with it.

EXERCISE 40.

From the very beginning you may feel only the general Qualities, let us say of cold, firm, poised closure. But this is only the beginning. Now you must repeat the same Psychological Gesture, but in a slightly changed manner. For instance, if the position of your head was previously straight, and your glance was also directed outward in front of you, lower your head slightly and glance downward. This change will bring certain nuances into your previous Qualities. Now you may feel a grim, stubborn shade mixed into the Qualities. Exercise this Gesture and the sentence until you can fulfill them freely. Do the first variation, then the second one. Compare them and appreciate the difference.

EXERCISE 41.

Proceed to the next change; it may be to slightly bend the knee of the right leg. Listen inwardly to this new nuance. Perhaps it contains a shade of despair and hopelessness. Let these Qualities enter into the sentence. Exercise them and compare them with the previous ones.

Join your hands higher, near your chin; lower your head more; close your eyes. Previous Qualities will become stronger. Lift your head and glance upward. A pleading nuance may be felt.

Now a further change. Turn your palms away from you. To the pleading Quality may now be added the Quality of self-protection. Incline your head on one side, and a sentimental nuance can be felt. Bend the two middle fingers of your hands. Listen to the humorous nuance in your Gesture.

The more you become sensitive to such alterations in your Gesture, the more imperceptible changes you must make. The position of your head and shoulders, your arms, hands, elbows, the turn of your neck and back, the position of your legs and feet, the direction of your glance, the position of your fingers, all will call up in your creative spirit corresponding Qualities and Feelings. Go on exercising this way until you feel that even the slightest idea of a possible change makes you react to it inwardly. You will also awaken in yourself the sense of harmony between outer and inner expressiveness in your acting—the feeling of scenic truth.

Having acquired this new ability, the actor can use it in his work to give a role more detail. He will see how, by applying this simple means, he will grow deeper and deeper into the complications that lie within the part.

Beyond the Limits of the Body

The weak and anemic Psychological Gesture cannot awaken the actor's Will and Feelings. Yet there is still the question of producing an exceptionally strong Gesture without unnecessary and disturbing physical tension. Let us suppose we energetically extend our arms, hands, and whole body to one side. This is our Psychological Gesture. In producing it powerfully, we may feel the limitations of our physical body rather than the real strength of the Gesture. The more we intensify the movement physically, the more strongly we experience the tension of our muscles and the inevitable contraction.

Our physical body has received a strong, inner impulse that threw it to one side, after which the physical movement stopped and the body became fixed. But the inner impulse, the initial activity, should not be stopped. It can and must go on, regardless of the body's inability to follow. Having physically completed the Psychological Gesture, we inwardly go on moving to the side. We do not need to tense our body for this. Quite the opposite: physical tension must be released, although not dropped entirely.

The first effort will show us that each Gesture can be continued inwardly as long as we wish. Whether we stretch out our hand and continue the imaginary stretching out or squeeze our fist tightly, in which case the activity itself seems to be fixed, there is no difference. The clenched fist obviously comes to a fixed state, but what prevents us from continuing the "clenching energy?" In our imagination we are free to clench our fist for any length of time.

Thus we are freed from the bonds of the physical body, and this activity is the actual strength of the Psychological Gesture. This internal activity is apt to awaken the actor's Will-impulse and the fire of his Feelings. This accumulated power is what ought to be used on the stage, never the illusionary power of tense muscles. Sufficient exercising will show the actor that psychological power is much greater than muscle power. He will also realize that it is psychological power that conveys to the audience all that he speaks, feels, does, and wishes as a character on the stage.

What about Gestures that must be soft, mild, and tender in their Qualities? Where does their power lie? There is no loss of power in mild Gestures. Such a question arises from the confusion of physical with psychological power. The inner activity in a mother's tender love, for instance, can be as strong as, and even stronger than, any violent activity. As soon as the actor becomes aware that the Psychological Gesture is an incessant movement and never a static position, he will realize that its activity is inclined to grow and its Qualities to become stronger and more expressive. So we may say that the real Psychological Gesture goes beyond the limits of the body.

IMAGINARY TIME AND SPACE

This new aspect of the Psychological Gesture will also give the actor new access to the elements of time and space. He can, for instance, extend his arm before him and move it from one side to the other in actual space and time, but he can also do it by extending his imaginary arm together with the real one to the horizon and moving it there for days and even years!

The actor can create a contracting Psychological Gesture of "curling up" into his body and even "disappearing" in his imagination. He can direct his Gesture down to the ground, and further down to the center of the earth. He can send his Gesture above his head into infinite space and experience there "fantastic" Feelings if he wishes. Or he can make an embracing, all-enclosing Gesture. In reality it will not take him more than five to eight seconds to do it physically, but he may extend it in his imagination to many "centuries." All the Qualities will begin to sparkle and live in a way worthy of being radiated to the audience. Look at our Feelings. All of them have a clearly expressed tendency to "break" the boundaries of actual time and space. Joy, love, and all kinds of excitement seem to live in "larger" space and "shorter" time than, for instance, sorrow, grief, and longing, which use "less" space and "longer" time.

There is a fantastic element in our Feelings and Will-impulses; the nonactor may not need to realize it for his everyday life, but the artist, the actor, must awaken the fantastic element within himself and make use of it. All movements, speech, "business"—all that the actor is going to do on the stage when the curtain is raised—will acquire new significance, charm, power, persuasiveness, and, most of all, an ineffable aura of true and genuine art. Even in the most naturalistic plays, in the most everyday business on the stage—reading a letter, drinking, eating, sitting calmly in a chair, putting on his overcoat—the actor will become an "actor-magician" who differs from the mere "actor-photographer" or "actor-reporter" whose accurate reflection of life seems more dull than life can ever be.

What the American designer Robert Edmund Jones wrote in his book, *The Dramatic Imagination,* about playwrights can also be applied to actors: "Instead of trying to raise us to the imaginative level of true dramatic creation, they have brought the theatre down to our own level." Again he wrote: "Everything that is actual must undergo a strange metamorphosis, a kind of sea-change, before it can become truth in the theatre." The fantastic element of the Psychological Gesture of the actor creates this metamorphosis.

This is not to say that all such Gestures have to be "eternal" and "infinite." It depends upon the theme, the kind of production, the scene, the moment, and most of all upon the taste and artistic tact of the actor himself. Here is the sphere of the actor's intuition, where rules and regulations have no place. The ability to work by means of fantastic Psychological Gestures and imaginary time and space elements is what matters. If the actor is an artist, he will know how to use these new, creative possibilities in order to preserve the spell of his art.

EXERCISE 42.

Choose any naturalistic position, for instance, lean with both hands on the table; sit in a chair with your head resting in your hands; lie on the couch with your hands under your neck; stand in the middle of the room with feet apart, hands behind your back, head slightly raised; lean your back against the wall, your head dropped on your arms, your face turned downward, and so on. Take any of these or similar positions before you realize what their psychological meaning may be. Then, holding the position, try to define what is expressed in it. What Qualities might be hidden behind such a position? What inner activity might have brought you to such a state? This psychological activity with the Qualities you have discovered must be continued inwardly by you. Concentrate completely on the radiation of the discovered activity with qualities, and do it until you feel that your inner strength grows, that the position is absolutely yours and that you can at any minute begin to improvise, starting from this position of yours. Then begin to improvise, continuing the position. You may speak words and do things freely, without any limitations. Go on improvising this way for a while, and then take another position.

EXERCISE 43.

Further development of this exercise requires a group of at least three people. One of the members of the group places the others in definite positions so that the whole group looks like a fixed moment in a scene that has been played and can be continued at any

moment. All the figures are connected with one another by the theme of the fixed scene. The person
who gives the positions for all the other members
must tell them what theme he or she has in mind.

For instance, the situation could be that of a group
of people around the bed of an ill or dying person;
or the pause at the end of a meeting, just before the
chairman speaks his concluding words and adjourns
the meeting; or a crowd of people reading a sensational announcement of a placard. Avoid positions
that may arise from, for instance, a suspended dance,
panic, or any rush. Such poses will create unnecessary
complications and distract attention. Having taken
their positions, the members of the group have to
explore and experience them just as we described
before for individual exercises. But this time, they
have to adjust their inner psychology, with their con-
tinuous activities and Qualities, to all other members
of the exercise. The outer adjustment was given, but
the inner harmony and coordination must be silently
found by each member, on his own. Then the "fixed"
scene continues in the form of a free improvisation
for a short time.

EXERCISE 44.

Now the member of the group who assigns the positions to the other members does not tell them what
the group theme is. The actors will have to discover
it by attentively exploring their own positions and by
penetrating the possible psychologies of the others.
Whether the group guesses exactly what was meant
by the distribution of the positions is immaterial. If
the scene continues harmoniously and sensibly, the
aim of the exercise has been achieved.

BETWEEN SCRIPT AND PERFORMANCE

All that we have said up to now about the Psychological Gesture can be summarized in the following way: the actor, starting his work on the play, finds himself between two poles. At one end is the written script and his role, at the other is his actual performance. There is a huge gap between the two, which is unknown and possibly obscure to the actor.

The play remains foreign to the performer until he knows how to act the content, or rather until he has the capacity to act it. Yet his acting cannot be stimulated until he knows or experiences the deeper level of the content of the play. If the actor begins rehearsals with theatrical clichés and old habits, his acting will follow a dead pattern. If he approaches the play by reading the author's words, without digging deeply behind them, his acquaintance with the play will be superficial and useless for the performance. The gap between the play and the acting will always remain large.

What can connect these two poles and thus fill the gap? Only the power of the actor's true individuality, which begins with his creative subconscious and artistic intuition. This is the only way to really explore the play, to find its deeper meaning, and to stimulate the acting, destroying all the clichés.

But is the "talent" of the actor always at his disposal? Can he command his subconscious at will? Does not the inspiration of the modern actor depend on his mood, his health, on the outer circumstances of his life, on hundreds of accidental things that are beyond his control? The actor must admit that he has no free access to his own talent unless he uses a special technique for it. The Psychological Gesture provides such a technique. Let us make it clear and explain it by means of a simple scheme.

The written play gives the actor the first ideas about the kind of Psychological Gestures, including their Qualities, he will need. By producing and exercising the Psychological Gesture suggested by the script, the actor approaches his subconscious creative powers. At this point, the Psychological Gestures absorb the music, rhythm, and beauty, the flame and the intensity of the thoughts and ideas of the actor's subconscious in their purest and most crystal-clear forms. The Psychological Gestures become rhythmical now. They resemble melodies rather than object- or action-based acting. Their Will-impulses, Qualities, and Atmospheres are not yet connected with any concrete objects; they are not yet factual acting.

From the time the creative powers of the actor are stirred and awakened by the work upon Psychological Gestures, his eyes are open to the play. He sees it more than before. He penetrates its depths and true significance. He begins to be moved by the content of the play and the character he is going to perform. At the same time, the actor feels that he grows and ripens inwardly more and more for his future performance. He no longer needs to refer to all sorts of clichés, but finds rather the source for his acting in his subconscious, which now begins to inspire him.

The "musical" Psychological Gestures transform themselves step by step into the acting, with all the words, business, objectives, score of Atmospheres, and situations given in the play and the character he is going to perform. While rehearsing and, later, onstage, the actor will always feel that the Psychological Gestures, which he discovered months earlier, stand constantly behind him, rendering to him that power and beauty, that charm and significance, that the Creative Individuality alone can give him.

The actor who is ready to accept our point of view should remember that all we have said must become a kind of sound "instinct" within him. Knowledge alone will not help him. He must need to go the right way, always moving by means of the Psychological Gesture, from the written play to the subconscious, and from there to factual acting. To develop such a constant and natural inclination, the actor has to exercise it patiently and regularly, even over a long period.

EXERCISE 45.

Listen to a piece of music, preferably one you know well, or recall a selection and listen to it in your imagination. While listening, try to imagine what kind of Psychological Gesture you can find to incorporate the inner movement of the music with its Quality. It is not important whether you take one musical phrase, or a series of them. Rather it is essential that you get inspiration for your Psychological Gesture from the source that is as remote from any naturalism as the music is. Rehearse it several times, then try to find another Psychological Gesture connected with the first. The music itself will be your guide. Rehearse the second Psychological Gesture, then produce both of them, following their inner musical connections. Do this until you are able to enjoy both of them in their inner, harmonious connection.

EXERCISE 46.

Execute both Psychological Gestures and then add a third Gesture, which now must be inspired not by the music, but solely by yourself. Let your third Gesture be born not only of the two previous ones, but of your own free inner impulse, your own sense of harmony, taste, and Feeling of Beauty. Now you have three Psychological Gestures. Start again from the first, then add the third, fourth, fifth, sixth, and so on, all on the basis of your free improvisation. Soon you will feel yourself so free that you will not need to start again from the first Gesture, but can go on indefinitely, adding one Psychological Gesture to the other, creating them and their organic connections spontaneously and entirely intuitively.

EXERCISE 47.

Try gradually and carefully to make your new Gestures resemble acting gestures more and more. Attempt more and more to give them a realistic, naturalistic character. By doing this slowly, step by step, you will have as a result a long chain of gestures whose first link will be a purely abstract, purely musical, rhythmical one, in close connection to your subconscious creative impulses, and whose last link will become the gesture of everyday life, concrete, and naturalistically true. The long series of gestures in between will be a slow transition from the "abstract" to the "concrete" gestures and words. You may use any short sentence, even from the very beginning. From the last link, start to develop an improvised "scene."

When you learn to do this long exercise uninterruptedly, you will come to the moment when your artistic nature itself will discover what actually is the process of transforming one's creative abilities into a concrete piece of art. The longer you do this exercise the more you will see rising in you a kind of wisdom about yourself as an artist, as an actor. Many small and great experiences, new and unfamiliar to you, will spring up in your soul, enriching and freeing your talent. The skillful managing of the technique of the Psychological Gesture will soon raise your acting standard, and will teach you to economize on time in preparing your part, but without succumbing to haste and deadening clichés.

CREATING CHARACTER THROUGH PSYCHOLOGICAL GESTURE

Long before I actually understood what the Psychological Gesture is, I had three seemingly insignificant experiences, the full meaning of which I was able to appreciate only much later.

While working upon the part of *Erik XIV* by August Strindberg at the Moscow Art Theatre's First Studio, I asked my director, Vakhtangov, many questions, trying to penetrate the very heart of the character and to grasp it all at once. Vakhtangov struggled with himself for a long time, endeavoring to find a satisfactory answer to my questions. One night at rehearsal he suddenly jumped up, exclaiming, "That is your Erik. Look! I am now within a magic circle and cannot break through it!" With his whole body he made one strong, painfully passionate movement, as though trying to break an invisible wall before him or to pierce a magic circle. The destiny, the endless suffering, the obstinacy, and the weakness of Erik XIV's character became clear to me. From that night I could act the part with all its innumerable nuances, through all four acts of the play.

Another experience I had was as follows: During one of the rehearsals of Nikolai Gogol's *The Inspector General*, Stanislavsky, the director of the play, while giving me his suggestions for the part of Khlestakov suddenly made a lightning-quick movement with his arms and hands, as if throwing them up and at the same time vibrating with his fingers, elbows, and even his shoulders. "That is the whole psychology of Khlestakov," said he laughingly (his gesture was indeed humorous). My soul was charmed by Stanislavsky's action and again I could set the whole part, just as in the previous case, from the beginning to the end without difficulty. I knew from then on how Khlestakov moved, spoke, felt, what he thought, how and what he desired, and so on.

The third experience was with Fyodor Chaliapin. Once he

was humorously teasing me, asking me questions about Stanislavsky's method and contradicting everything I said (having at the same time a genuine interest in Stanislavsky's System). "Well," he said, "according to 'your' method you can produce miracles on the stage, can't you? You can even make out of such a tall, big man as myself a small, tiny figure? Is it not so?" And here he made a movement with his whole majestic body and, to my great astonishment, I saw before me for a moment a tiny little man with a small, thin body.

Thus, three great masters have shown me unwittingly three brilliant Psychological Gestures! What these masters did in moments of inspiration, we contemporary actors can learn to do, in order that we may be able to use it as one of the means of our professional technique. And it can be learned by anyone who was born with even the merest spark of talent.

Each character on the stage has one main desire, and one characteristic manner of fulfilling this desire. Whatever variations the character may show during the play in pursuing his main desire, he nevertheless always remains the same character. We know that the desire of the character is his Will ("what"), and his manner of fulfilling it is its Quality ("how"). Since the Psychological Gesture is composed of the Will, permeated with the Qualities, it can easily embrace and express the complete psychology of the character.

Through his imagination, through acting with Qualities and other means, the actor digs deeper and deeper into his character. His final aim is to absorb the character in its entirety. This work can be done simultaneously with the attempt, with the series of attempts, to create a Psychological Gesture for the character as a whole. The actor can endeavor to find such a Gesture at any stage of his work, be it late or early. The technique of applying the Psychological Gesture in this case is exactly the same as was described before in other cases. What the actor needs to be able to achieve this aim is sufficient skill and experience, which he can develop by exercising.

EXERCISE 48.

Concentrate at first on the simple realization of the fact that the Psychological Gesture is composed of a Will-impulse painted by Qualities. Move your arm and body in a certain direction. Realize that your Will finds its expression through this movement. Then add to this Will Movement any Quality you choose, for instance "joyfully," "suspiciously," "stubbornly," "decisively," and so on. Realize that in this simple form you have the whole construction of the Psychological Gesture.

Now start to combine different gestures with different Qualities and exercise each of them long enough to be able to do any simple naturalistic business, having this Psychological Gesture behind you as a kind of guide or inspiration for all your simple, everyday business. If your Psychological Gesture was, for instance, cowardly aggression, so all your business must be permeated with the aggressive but cowardly Will.

EXERCISE 49.

Try to find an outer characterization for the chosen Psychological Gesture: the posture of your body, the kind of movements you use, your manner of speech, and imaginary makeup. Go on improvising business and words for this character. Try to imagine it on the stage before your mind's eye, the same way you do with any other character taken from a play. In this way you will give your newly born character a kind of independent life. Develop the character in your imagination as much and as long as you wish.

You can accomplish such an exercise in one day, or you can return to it for a longer period of time. The essence of the exercise is to experience the Psychological Gesture becoming a complete character.

EXERCISE 50.

Think of different people whom you know well and try to discover for yourself what kind of Psychological Gesture would express their Will and its main Qualities. Try to imitate them in their everyday life, always aiming at the Psychological Gesture that expresses the whole character of the person you have chosen for your investigation. Never show the result of your work to the persons who have unwittingly rendered you their help.

Choose any character from a play or a novel (Dickens's characters are the most suitable material for such work) and start imagining it. Try, as before, to discover the Psychological Gesture for the chosen character. Having found it begin to exercise it and gradually come to the words and business described by the author.

At first you will have more success creating Psychological Gestures for characters without partners. If your improvisation requires other people, you can easily imagine them, leading your dialogues with them as though they were present. Create Psychological Gestures for every aspect of your character while watching other actors on the stage or in the movies.

Continue your exercises in the following way: Look at unknown people on the street and try instantly to find in your imagination the Psychological Gesture of their characters. The first fleeting impression you get from such unknown people passing you on the street must be the only ground for your lightning-quick discovery. Don't expect immediate success from such exercises. Continue for the sake of the exercise itself. Here, as always, the effort is what matters.

OTHER BENEFITS

As soon as the actor begins to appreciate and then to love working with Psychological Gestures, he will see that there is no longer any need for floundering and groping at random in the dark. All stages of his work will be filled with the reasonable application of the Psychological Gesture. His professional work will become sure, exact, and rapid. Besides, he will feel from his own experience that he is now more original and individual in his work than before, because the Psychological Gesture can only be really produced in an entirely individual way. It cannot be imitated at all, even when suggested from the outside, by the director, for example.

An actor can try very hard to copy a Psychological Gesture that someone else has shown him, but he will soon be convinced that unless he fills this outside Psychological Gesture with his own Will and his own individual Qualities, the Psychological Gesture will mean nothing at all, even less than a cliché. This is so because the Psychological Gesture is the nearest thing to the actor's Creative Individuality.

Another benefit of the Psychological Gesture is the positive effect it will have on the actor's taste, which will develop and become more refined. Deep in his talented nature the actor is irreproachable in his taste; what spoils it—even from childhood—is either vulgar, rude, and ungraceful impressions of his surroundings or, later on, a superficial, unscrupulous, negligent, and hasty way of expressing himself on the stage. The Psychological Gesture in the actor's profession is the means of receiving impressions by exploring the part, and at the same time of expressing his artistic conceptions in their first imprint. In both cases the Individuality itself supervises these processes. It purifies them by giving them its elegance.

The vitality and power of the actor's expressiveness on the stage will also grow. The Psychological Gesture, which possesses spiritual power rather than physical strength, enables the actor to renounce all sorts of pushing, forcing, pressing, and straining in his acting. These signs of the actor's weakness usually lead to overacting rather than expressiveness. Therefore, the actor must not be afraid of producing the Psychological Gesture as strongly as he can, knowing that this strength will later on stand behind him, making his acting expressive without exaggeration.

The Psychological Gesture also makes the actor approach his work consciously. He knows what he does and takes full account of each step he undertakes. But the kind of consciousness we speak of here is entirely different from what he would use to try to analyze his part in a dry, intellectual way. The Psychological Gesture stands in the middle, between vague floundering and arid reasoning. It is the product of pure, sound imagination. For this conscious work the actor will find himself greatly rewarded by the rich inflow of inspiration from his subconscious.

6

INCORPORATION
AND
CHARACTERIZATION

Players are the only
honest hypocrites.
HAMLET

INCORPORATION

The actor imagines with his body. He cannot avoid gesturing or moving without responding to his own internal images. The more developed and stronger the image, the more it stimulates the actor to physically incorporate it with his body and voice. On this natural ability of the actor we base our principle of Incorporation.

Let us say that the actor has visualized a character in his imagination that he is going to perform on the stage. It gradually becomes clearer in his mind's eye. A desire to physicalize it grows. What shall he do to achieve his aim? It would be wrong to force his body to fully incorporate the image because that would cause an immediate shock to his system. The effort would be physically short-circuited.

The first bodily expression would not be like the internal image. The actor would be compelled to be untruthful in his means of expression to create the character-image. Performers will frequently mobilize all their habits of speaking and moving in order to pretend that their old worn-out clichés are just what the character needs. Instead of these banal means the actor should look upon the character in his imagination, seeing it moving, hearing it speaking, thus displaying its inner life before his mind's eye. He should first fix his attention on one chosen feature. He should study it attentively in his imagination and then try to incorporate only this one feature.

Let us say that the actor sees the character moving its hands. He studies this and then incorporates the movement as if imitating it. After doing this several times, the imaginary movement will gradually achieve a faithful expression in the movement of his own hands. He can continue doing so until his own psychological and physical makeup changes and becomes more suitable for the character. Proceeding in this manner he will in the end embrace the whole character in a single grip. The aim is achieved. The careful incorporation of separate features is no longer necessary, but the actor can return to this work again later on in case he partly loses the character. At that point such Incorporation will serve to direct him again on the right path.

The actor can exercise the technique of Incorporation on any image he chooses. The finer the image the more valuable is the result of Incorporation, and the richer will be the acting later on.

LEADING QUESTIONS

There is a way to refine the well-trained imagination and deepen the means of Incorporation. It is the method of Leading Questions. But whom can the actor question? He may question his image, just as he would a friend. He will receive an answer if his imagination is flexible and courageous. Instead of guessing whether the character wants to cry or to hide its feelings, to move or remain immovable, to use this or that nuance while entering a room, what tempo to use in this or that speech, and so on, the actor asks his image to act before his mind's eye, and to show him all possible variations and nuances.

The actor chooses freely and objectively from what he has seen. The image rehearses for him, being led by his questions. The finest and most subtle questions will find response in a well-developed imagination. Thus, leading his image by means of questioning, the actor will see what the director's, the author's, and his own desires look like. The more experienced the actor becomes in questioning, the more subtle details will begin to sparkle in his imagination. In most cases such Leading Questions kindle real and rich inspiration in the actor. This means of refining his imagination, in order to incorporate the subtleties of the character, can be exercised by the actor on any chosen image.

CHARACTERIZATION THROUGH INCORPORATION

A well-developed Imagination, Leading Questions, a sensitive body, and the method of Incorporation bring us directly to the next point of our method—Characterization. How many actors fall victim to the error of submitting to clichés in their work! There are clichés for the ingenue, the hero, elderly characters; for funny, dramatic, or stupid characters; for wise or simple characters, and so on. I don't think that the actor himself really believes that the whole of humanity can be reduced to so many clichés, but on the stage he very often makes this reduction. He loses his ability to observe real life, and forgets that there are individuals around him.

Rudolf Steiner said, "Again and again one meets actors

who don't really know the world. However, they know the characters in Shakespeare's, Goethe's, and Schiller's writings well. They know William Tell, Hamlet, Macbeth, Richard III. They know the whole world as a reflection of dramatic literature, but they don't know real people." This is a grave truth.

The actor must seek refuge from his worst enemy, clichés, by a constant and sharp observation of living people with their characteristic and individual manners. He must observe greedily how a person puts his foot on the ground, what is his favorite gesture, why he uses it, how he polishes his spectacles and why he doesn't put them on immediately, how he hides his embarrassment, how he listens with interest to himself talking but is bored when listening to others speak, and so forth.

But the actor must notice the other person's characteristic features with humor and not with criticism. He must form the habit of making such observations; then, when the circumstances allow, he must try to imitate, to incorporate all the characteristic features he has accumulated during his observations. This valuable material will be stored in the actor's subconscious and, being forgotten, will appear of itself when needed, in a transformed, individualized way. It will enrich and stir the actor's inventiveness and surely will cure him of his clichés. It will teach him to see things that others don't see.

Max Reinhardt, whose natural powers of observation were extremely strong, told me at our first meeting—having observed me no longer than five minutes—what part I had wanted so eagerly to act for many years. How did he know? Under the training of observation, the actor's imagination will acquire more variety and his humor will also grow. Sooner or later, the actor will come to the firm conviction that there are no parts without characterization, however slight and delicate they may be. He will cease once and for all acting himself in his appearances on the stage. He will be embarrassed to act himself, because he will feel as though he were naked, as though his profession were too insignificant and too easy. Could it not be that Robert Edmund Jones had just such actors in mind when he wrote, "Some actors have even made me feel at times that they were at heart a little bit ashamed of being actors"?

The more specific the role, the more it is removed from the actor's own bodily appearance in the majority of cases. Of course, Falstaff cannot be produced by a young, thin boy; neither can Joan of Arc be acted by a heavy, elderly lady. There are limits given by the nature of the actor's body, but there are also possibilities for the actor to change his body to a much greater extent than one might think who has not experienced it himself. Again there is the question of the right and wrong approach to this problem.

If, for instance, a young, thin man tries to become fat and imposing on the stage by the outer means of putting padding on his body, he might not be able to overcome either his physical or psychological difficulties. He will not be persuasive for the audience because of his inner, untruthful attitude. This approach is so obviously wrong that actors of the present time often try to avoid such artificiality by either evading parts that cannot be portrayed correctly with their own bodies and their own faces or by narrowing down all the parts to their own bodily capacities. But this is not the solution. Would not such an actor resemble the sailor who sets the same sail for all breezes? No true actor can be persuaded that his profession consists of continuously repeating himself every time he has to act a new part. The desire and the ability to transform oneself are the very heart of the actor's nature.

IMAGINARY BODY WITH ITS CENTER

What means can we suggest for truthfully changing our bodies as much as possible? Here again the actor has to appeal to his imagination. Let us say that he has to become, on the stage, taller and thinner than he is in reality. The first step he must take is to imagine, as it were, another body for himself, create an Imaginary Body that is taller and thinner than his own. But he must imagine this within his real, visible body, occupying the same space. He must imagine this Imaginary, or Invisible, Body many times until he gets a clear picture of it.

The next step will be a careful process of putting the actor's body into the Imaginary Body, trying to move the physical body so that it will follow the characteristic movements and shape of the Imaginary one. If the actor lifts up his imaginary long lean arm, he also moves his real arm within it. Exercising in this way, the actor will find that the manner in which he moves his real arm begins to convey the impression that it is long and lean. Without yet using any outer means, he will create the impression that he has another arm by his movement alone. Thus the actor acquires other legs, another back, neck, and finally re-creates his whole body, limb by limb.

Gradually the necessity of imagining the Invisible Body will disappear. This was only a preliminary, preparatory stage. A new experience in his own, real body will substitute for the imaginary one. Now he can help himself by creating the characteristic costume that will accentuate the necessary features of the character. Even padding, if necessary, is now permissible. The actor will no longer lie inwardly by using these externals.

The Imaginary Body can be elaborated on very finely and with many details. To this refinement the actor must add the imaginary Center about which we spoke earlier. The imaginary Center gives the whole body a harmonious appearance because, being in the middle of the chest, it draws the character nearer to the ideal body. But now we shall consider this Center from the point of view of characterization.

As soon as the actor moves this Center to another place in his body, the ideal body changes and acquires a defined countenance. For instance, the actor can put the Center in his head, in which case he may feel that his mind becomes more active and begins to play a specific part in his whole inner and outer makeup. This general application of the Center, placed in the actor's head, will undergo innumerable variations according to the type of character the actor is going to portray.

If Faust is to be portrayed, for instance, the Center in the head will enable the actor to perform Faust's wisdom, but if he is to play Wagner, Faust's friend, the Center may help him to express fanatical narrow-mindedness. More nuances will come if the actor will freely imagine the Center quite differently in various cases. The Center in Faust's head, for instance, can be a fairly big one, light and radiating, while Wagner's might be imagined as a contracted, small, and even hard Center. The Center can be placed anywhere: in the shoulder; in one of the eyes (e.g., Tartuffe or Quasimodo); in the stomach (Falstaff, Sir Toby Belch); in the knees (Aguecheek), which may create a humorous outer as well as psychological characterization; in front of the body (Prospero, Hamlet, Othello); behind the back (Sancho Panza). All variations imaginable are possible and correct if the actor finds them in accordance with his own and his director's interpretation of the part.

As an example, let us imagine that the actor is to perform the part of Don Quixote. From the very beginning of his work he has used his imagination and now he goes on tracing the adventures of that glorious knight. The task the actor now sets himself is to draw out of his visions some characteristic features of Quixote himself. Wherever he sees him, whether standing on guard with his weapons or riding horseback through the desert at night or espying Mambrino's helmet, he sees that Quixote's senses are strained, his consciousness opened and widened, as his mind searches throughout the earth seeking for hidden wicked magicians— they are watching for him and he is watching for them. His quick thoughts, palpitating heart, and stubborn will have become accessible to the actor almost from the beginning through his vital imagination. The actor starts questioning the image.

"While standing guard, show me the positions of your head, neck, and shoulders."

The helmeted figure begins to change slightly, scarcely noticeably, as if being molded from inside. The shoulders drop, the neck stretches upward more and more, trying to lift the restless, troubled head higher and higher, as if to reach the sparkling Center whirling high above it. The image is like a gigantic, absurd, lonely bird on the watch!

"Show me your face."

The eyes open wide and look far off, unseeing. The thin, matted beard sticks out, pointing to distant, unknown places. The lips mutter curses and threats at the ravishers, prayers for the victims.

"Show me your arms and hands."

From the drooping shoulders they hang down helplessly. Long, long arms. Heavy, idle hands. Childlike, splayed fingers. Pointed elbows. The Imaginary Body molds all this for the actor in answer to his Leading Questions.

"Show me your legs and feet!"

A sudden, strong Will-impulse straightens the thin legs of the "bird on the watch." He is ready to make a wide bound in order to finish off a sorcerer, wizard, or witch with one stroke! The more the old legs strain themselves the more the knees protrude. They are just like the elbows, but point in the other direction. Heavily armed but patched, the shoes bear the whole weight of the lean, lanky apparition on their heels. The toes point upward. The possible construction of the Imaginary Body becomes clearer and clearer for the actor.

"Now, the enemy is in view!"

In no time all is changed! The Center, "the watchtower," drives down at full speed and stops in the middle of the body, bends it in two, throws both shoulders high, together with the arms and hands. One of the gloves with fewer fingers flies high up.

"Attack!"

What is that? The armed figure jumps toward the enemy . . . backward . . . (why not forward?) . . . two, three steps . . . then turns . . . then again and again. The Center (now small and dark) shoots cautiously back and forth . . . (but why backward?). The actor knows why better than the knight himself . . . (isn't he within him?). There is too much suspicion, guessing, surmising, in the old knight's nature!

"Now for the important characteristic feature, suspicion! Show me more of that."

At a table in a tavern sits a helmeted figure, upright, bloater in hand. To the right sits chomping Sancho. Opposite is the princess (the harlot). At the figure's left sits the red-faced host. Who is he? Sage? Conjurer? Nobleman of high birth? Grandee? Wretch? Quixote looks to the right, eyes running, the left shoulder up, the right eyebrow raised, lips tightened . . . worried . . . guessing. The whole thin Imaginary Body is angular, asymmetrical, all awry, sticking out; its Center spins around the host, poking and thrusting at him . . . suspicious!

We see a valley at dawn . . . distant noise . . . threatening . . . low . . . growling. Is it a band of carefree magicians? Let them come! The knight turns his ear toward them and at the same time turns his whole heavily armored figure away . . . the right direction is lost for a while. The Center, high up in the chest, becomes larger and larger, disturbing the beating of the heart and the breathing until it is ready to burst. The Invisible Body lengthens in the legs, but grows and swells in the chest. The eyebrows fly up, the neck draws into the shoulders. The spear is clutched in the hand. The "bird" is about to fly up, suspicious, alarmed!

Now, at home at La Mancha. He is ill, wounded, exhausted. Careful steps are heard behind the door again and again. Is it the housekeeper, niece, physician, minister? Who knows? Quixote, stretched out in bed under the blanket, all flat, as if ironed out, shoots his Center across his small room, diagonally, and hangs it, like a feebly flickering lantern, above the door. The head and eyes are turned away, as always when guessing. The Imaginary Body, even weaker than the real one, draws the physical body down and down, both becoming flatter and flatter . . . doubtful . . . restless.

Such free playing with the Invisible Body and the Center, while imagining, makes it clear for the actor what the characterization can really be. Although it is movable, flexible, fantastically fluid, it can nevertheless be established somehow for the whole character. For instance, Don Quixote could have his tall, thin Invisible Body with the Center high above his head as a constant, typical form.

Such an Imaginary Body, with its Center, strongly entices the actor to perform, just as does the Psychological Gesture. The molding and driving power is within and behind the image. As soon as the image crystalizes itself before the actor's mind's eye, the Invisible Body can be applied in all the creative stages of work that follow.

By means of our example we also wish to touch upon the necessity for the actor, while looking for the characterization, to appeal first to the psychological makeup of the character. The outer features will always follow. The Psychological Gesture, the Imaginary Body, and the Center are nothing other than the link between the psychology and the outer means of expression of the actor.

The proper exercising of the Imaginary Body and the Center will make them absolutely necessary for the actor, will give him pleasure and joy, and will become a kind of habit in the creative approach to his work. Having arrived at this stage of development, the actor will for the first time be able to really appreciate the value of these points of technique and realize how much time and energy he will be able to save by applying them to his creative work.

EXERCISE 51.

Think of any form of the Imaginary Body you choose. Think of your own body as being inside of it. Arbitrarily put the imaginary Center anywhere in the Imaginary Body. Visualize them as clearly as possible. Give the Body and the Center any Qualities you wish. Remember that the Center can be imagined freely without any restrictions as large, small, changing in size, movable, swinging, revolving, departing, approaching, and so forth. Now realize what kind of character you have. In this exercise, as you see, you have to go backward from the Body and the Center, arbitrarily combined to create the psychology of the character.

Now try to move in character. Do this until you feel entirely free in it. Begin to improvise some suitable words or sentences, having found the correct manner of speech. Now add some business, which can be simple but appropriate. Do this until you become free enough to enjoy your character with its speech and business. Make slight alterations in the Imaginary Body and Center. Follow carefully and attentively these alterations, which will result in the psychology of the character.

EXERCISE 52.

Choose a character from a play or literary work. This time follow the path from the psychology to the Invisible Body and Center. Start with the imagining of the chosen character. When the character becomes clear to you, start to incorporate it bit by bit. Having achieved freedom in the incorporated character—there is no need to incorporate the character through the whole play—start to find its characteristic features.

EXERCISE 53.

Give yourself the task of creating five different characters in half an hour, one after the other. Try in this short period of time to make them as rich, as full, as you can. Try to find their Imaginary Bodies and characteristic Centers. Find their speech and typical actions. Repeat this exercise day after day, once a day, until you are able to do it easily. Then shorten the time to twenty-five minutes, then to twenty minutes. Do not elaborate on your characters, do not return to them next day, but leave them in a sketchy form.

7

FROM
SCRIPT
TO
REHEARSAL HALL

*It must always be kept in mind
that it is not necessary to learn
what you are already able to judge.
Therefore, if one only wants to judge
things, one cannot learn anymore
at all.*
RUDOLF STEINER

THE OBJECTIVE

The Objective was invented by Konstantin Stanislavsky and is described in his book *An Actor Prepares.* Briefly, the Objective is concerned with the problem of how to compose the actor's Will-impulses on the stage in connection with the play's content. Everyone is always wishing something, always has a goal. This goal directs all a person's actions, conduct, and words. In life, many aims are woven into a complicated psychological whole, much of which dwells in the half-conscious or even subconscious regions of the person. But for the actor on the stage, conveying the Objective of the character must be a conscious effort.

Knowing the Objective, the actor directs his acting so that the text and business lead to the achievement of the Objective. Such aiming on the part of the character makes the acting sensible and gives the play a strong spine. A conscious Objective, maintained during the period of rehearsal, gradually becomes unconscious and thus influences the actor's conduct on the stage. We wish to add some suggestions as to how the Objective can be used.

TWO WAYS OF FINDING THE OBJECTIVE

It is too easy and, therefore, too enticing to define the Objective by means of dry, intellectual analysis. In this case, the danger lies in the difficulty of transmitting the Objective from the purely mental sphere to the region of the actor's Will, where it belongs. It is a peculiarity of the intellect to conserve in its region things that it has understood. There they become cold and inactive. The Objective thus captured by the intellect cannot be of use to the actor. All that he undertakes on the stage with such an intellectually understood Objective will become artificial, thought out, poor, and surely misleading.

First, one needs the imagination in order to find the Objective. This means that the actor sees his character acting before his mind's eye and, while observing it, endeavors to guess what the Objective may be. By watching the vivid pictures of his imagination actively, and not by reasoning alone, the actor may expect to solve the problem of the Objective. To see the Objective before knowing it is his aim. "There is an outer eye that observes, and there is an inner eye that sees," wrote Robert Edmund Jones, and it is to this inner eye that the actor appeals when searching for the Objective by means of imagining. He may be sure that he will not fail in this search if he does not try impatiently to force the result. The process of experiencing through the imagination cannot be violated. It is useless and dangerous to try because the intellect is always on the lookout. Having been found this way, the Objective comes as a pleasant revelation, urging the actor's Will, which reasoning can never do.

The second way of finding the Objective is this: Act spontaneously several times, then as yourself ask, "What have I done? What was I aiming at?" This is to search for the Objective by appealing to one's Will. Here again, before knowing what the Objective is, we experience it. While freely acting so many moments or scenes, the actor must keep a "spying eye" upon himself. Whether the answer comes while you are acting or afterward, it will arise from the realm of your Will, avoiding the sphere of your intellectual reasoning. You can do this easily while incorporating bits of your part, or you can start acting for the purpose of finding the Objective only. In this case, you do not have to act fully, as you would if you were before an audience. You will get the desired result even by merely hinting at your probable acting—by speaking and moving on the sly. This can be done alone or with partners. By taking simple and obvious Objectives, you must make sure that they do not remain only in your mental sphere, because of their obviousness.

TO FIX AND ELABORATE ON THE OBJECTIVE

In both of these suggested means of finding the Objective, the mission of the intellect is to understand and to fix what has been already found. But the best way to fix, refine, and exercise the Objective is by means of the Psychological Gesture. The only way for the intellect to fix the Objective is to find a verbal formulation for it: "I wish to . . ."

This becomes a symbol for the Objective, but not the Objective itself, whereas the Psychological Gesture, as the crystalized Will, is the Objective. A verbal symbol cannot be exercised by the actor, but can only remind him of what has to be exercised and developed. The Psychological Gesture, though, can undergo any kind of elaboration, growth, and development. Each "I wish to . . ." can be turned into a Psychological Gesture.

TO POUR THE OBJECTIVE OUT INTO THE BODY

As we have said before, the Psychological Gesture occupies the whole body, the whole being of the actor, and so will the Objective when turned into such a Gesture. For instance, when the mother embraces the child, having perhaps the Objective to "merge with" (Psychological Gesture) the being she loves more than herself, it is felt in her legs, arms, and whole body. A person who is afraid and wants to escape (the Psychological Gesture) the object of his fear feels the impulse for escape in all his limbs and in his whole body, down to the very tips of his fingers. The very weary person who sits on a chair with the Objective to get up (the Psychological Gesture) feels the desire to get up in all his limbs long before he is able to do so. If the actor's body and whole being have not felt the experience of being tangibly filled with certain Will content, as in the case with the Psychological Gesture, then he can be sure that he has not yet found the real Objective—this guiding and inspiring impulse within him.

OBJECTIVE AS A PICTURE

If a mother desires to hold her child to her bosom, in her vision she is already doing so. If a weary person wishes to get up from the armchair, in his imagination he is getting up. Leo Tolstoy said that if someone is haunted by the desire for revenge, he is stimulated by pictures of punishment. They increase and strengthen his Objective. But he need only replace such pictures with others and his Objective will change. If he tries to see the other person completely defeated, severely punished, and crushed, his Objective will give place to another, perhaps a desire to forgive, to help, to reconcile. The actor can use such pictures for his Objectives, choosing them freely in accordance with his part and the situations in the play.

For example, "I wish to snatch his secret from him" might be the Objective. Through many scenes, perhaps even through the whole play, the character may cherish such a general Objective. But in each scene he might be given different means, different opportunities "to snatch" that secret. This gives the actor rich material for imagining several concrete but different pictures in the fulfillment of his Objective. Supposing that the character with the above-mentioned Objective meets another in a crowded room. The first character looks for the opportunity to have an immediate conversation with the other. His Objective urges him to do this. Into the actor's mind at this moment may flash a picture of himself and the other character having such a talk—indicating that the concrete picture of the Objective is in the process of its fulfillment. The picture becomes an urging, inspiring power in the actor's will.

TO TAKE AND DROP THE OBJECTIVE

When exercising and using the Objective in rehearsal, we must, having fulfilled it, drop it completely without retaining any indefinite impulses and vague reminders of it. Otherwise, the actor's performance will take on a flattened, linear shape. The clearer the initial and final stages of the utilization of the Objective, however, the more strongly the actor will be able to experience it and then drop it.

EXERCISE 54.

Take any short scene from a play. Find one or several sentences and some business belonging to the character, then act, trying to discover the Objective.

EXERCISE 55.

Observe unknown people around you. Try to guess what their Objectives might be at the moment of your observation.

EXERCISE 56.

Take a simple Objective—to go out of the room; to touch a chosen object; to remove a chair; or to open to a certain page in a book—and fulfill it. Do it as many times as necessary to really experience the driving power of an Objective.

EXERCISE 57.

Choose a sentence and some business. For instance, take a letter from your partner's hand with the words "Don't send that letter now, it may be dangerous!" The partner can be either real or imaginary. Let your Objective be to prevent the sending of the letter. Fulfill it by different means, by persuading, by commanding, by imploring, by frightening, by threatening, by flattering, and so forth. See that your words and movements are in harmony with each other and really help the Objective.

Now create simple, short improvisations with Objectives and Atmospheres.

ACTIVITY

Through strong concentration and a vivid imagination, together with the use of the Psychological Gesture behind the acting, Rudolf Steiner's Eurythmy and Speech Formation, the Objective and the Atmosphere, the actor will experience something resembling a process of awakening. His inner Activity will increase and will seek an outlet. A constant impulse for creative work will be present in him. He will feel that everything he does on the stage is accomplished easily and reaches his audience. How often the actor on the stage pushes out his words, feelings and movements, without having any real impulse for it, hoping that the impulse will come mechanically. This is the wrong kind of Activity. He pushes instead of letting the words, feelings, and movements flow on the natural, intrinsic wave of Activity.

What is the difference between these two kinds of activity? The incorrect one is nearly always restricted to a certain part of our being, whether it is the speech apparatus or the limbs that we move. The correct Activity is not located anywhere. This Activity permeates the whole being, psychologically as well as physically. If the incorrect Activity seeks to form habits that become theatrical clichés, correct activity seeks always for new and fresh means of expression and cannot allow clichés, which automatically manacle it.

Incorrect Activity exhausts us quickly, while correct Activity fills us with new life and a new desire to create. Whereas incorrect Activity causes contraction in our body and soul, correct Activity frees us and leads to expansion. The actor must discriminate between the two kinds of Activity in himself, and must try always to keep to the right one. The hampering powers in us always diminish and dampen proper Activity, but having once found it, the actor must endeavor to maintain it.

It is important to understand that there are three degrees of Activity in our consciousness—dreaming, waking, and creating. The last is, of course, the highest and strongest. The creative state should be activated in the actor even during rehearsals. The actor should not believe that he may appear on the stage with the same degree of Activity as he possesses in his private life. This wrong belief prevents him from realizing that on the stage the level of his private life appears lower than it appears in his everyday existence. With a desire to look natural, he gives the impression of a lifeless puppet. He lacks the increased degree of Activity, which alone can enable the actor to look "as in life" from the audience.

This cannot be proved logically, and must be left to the intuition of the actor to see with his own eyes. Here are the words of the French actor, Constant Coquelin: "You as an actor are in the theatre and not on the street or at home. If you put on the stage the action of the street or the home, these will resemble very much what would happen if you were to put a life-sized statue on top of a column: It would no longer seem to be life-sized." The audience and the critics have become accustomed to such unnatural naturalism on the modern stage, and therefore, their judgment cannot be considered as offering guidance.

The actor sometimes feels himself so comfortable, so irresponsibly at ease on the stage, that he swims in coziness and is even in danger of becoming languid. He is acting just as though he were at home. In this case, whose "simplicity" are we forced to see on the stage? The actor's? We are not interested in it. But where is the character? It is drowned in the actor's personal simplicity. But should not the character be simple? Yes, of course. It is the greatest achievement to be able to show Hamlet, Lear, Prospero, Lady Macbeth, Juliet, or Othello with the utmost simplicity. These characters must become human and not dead, empty figures! Then they will appear simple on the stage. But the actor can only find this simplicity behind their great words and deeds if he will sacrifice his personal "simplicity." The simplicity of the character is the result of increased activity and may involve very complicated preliminary work for the actor. The character must be always present on the stage. This is an axiom.

RADIATION

As a result of keeping to the right kind of Activity, the actor will find that he has acquired the ability to Radiate out of himself emotions, Feelings, Will-impulses, and Images while on the stage. He will appreciate this ability as one of the strongest means of expression, and as soon as he becomes aware of it, he can support and increase it by means of his conscious effort. His habit of concentration will also strengthen this ability.

On the stage the actor will feel himself as a kind of center that continuously expands in any and all directions he chooses. More than this, the actor will be able, through the power of Radiation, to convey to the audience the finest and most subtle nuances of his acting, and the deepest meaning of the text and situations. In other words, the audience will receive the contents of the scenic moment together with the actor's most intimate and individual interpretation of it.

If the Atmosphere bears the content in general, then Radiation bears it in detail. Let us take an example: King Claudius attends the performance that Hamlet has arranged for him. The general Atmosphere of the scene is that of increasing tension, preceding a disaster. The play goes on. In Claudius's guilty conscience, chaotic powers rise higher and higher. The climax approaches. The tension bursts. "The King rises!" cries Ophelia. But the horror-stricken King, the center of all attention, calls out, "Give me some light! Away!" and leaves the stage. That is all.

If the actor who portrays King Claudius wishes to rely upon the words and their meaning only, he will undoubtedly find himself in great difficulty. Fear, hatred, remorse, a wild impulse to run away and yet not lose his high dignity, thoughts of revenge and hastily formed plots to put them off the scent, and the inability to grasp the new situation—the actor must convey these and many other things to his audience at this climactic moment. How can he do all this, with few words of such poor content, and such a primitive action as sudden flight? Then all the richness of Claudius's "hell" will be lost for the audience.

It will surely be lost if a strong, overwhelming flow of Radiation does not take place at such a critical moment in the play. If all that turns King Claudius in this scene into a wild yet noble animal is present in the soul of an actor who possesses the ability of Radiation, it will be flung into the audience in an instant, regardless of the meager words and poor business. More than that, such Radiation will make the words and the business highly significant and impressive. Those indescribable, unspeakable things that the actor has accumulated in his soul while working creatively on his part will be conveyed only through Radiation. So an intangible means of expression may become the most tangible part of the performance, revealing the play, the part, and the actor's individual face behind them.

Although we have said that Activity and with it Radiation will come of themselves, it is possible through exercises to quicken the process of an actor's development and to strengthen both abilities.

EXERCISE 58.

Define a line on the floor as if it were the threshold of a door which you have to cross. Approach it from the distance, keeping in mind that while crossing it you have, through a sudden impulse, to increase your Activity as much as you can. Do this many times until you are sure that you do not strain your muscles instead of producing a psychological flash of Activity. By doing this correctly you will experience a sudden expansion, whereas tense muscles will only cause inner contraction.

Now, add to this sudden flash of Activity a strong impulse to radiate from your chest straight out in front of you. Avoid any tension of the muscles. Vary the manner of radiating. Stretch out your arm, pointing at some definite spot; look sharply at some point, radiating from your eyes; radiate from your forehead; open your arms and hands, radiating from your palms; radiate while moving your hand from one point in the room to the other; do the same with your glance, with your whole figure, and so on.

EXERCISE 59.

Until now you were radiating your Activity in a very general way. Now take some Quality (or Feeling); approach the threshold and make the Gesture, radiating the Quality you have chosen. Do this with different variations. Find a word or sentence for the chosen Quality and speak it, radiating it and the Gesture together.

EXERCISE 60.

Try to awaken your Activity and power of Radiation while remaining physically immobile. Do this several times. Radiate from definite parts of your body, always in a single direction.

EXERCISE 61.

Find a concrete action and fulfill it, trying to follow your active Radiations without defining them beforehand. Do it first without any definite Qualities, then with Qualities, and finally with words. Proceed to improvisations (alone or with partners). Do not give any attention to Activity or to Radiation, but let them appear in you unconsciously, on their own.

SIGNIFICANCE

As the natural result of Activity and Radiation, the actor's work will become significant in all his moments on the stage. This fact is even more important for the success of the performance as a whole than for the actor himself.

Let us imagine that on the stage an event of importance has taken place, but the actors convey it insignificantly to the audience. The important moment becomes unnecessary, it loses its connection with the gist of the play. The performance loses its harmony and the idea of the play is obscured. But the same, or even worse, happens if the actor conveys an event of secondary importance too significantly. Such a mistake entirely confuses the audience's perception of the whole performance. The spectators instinctively neglect the performance as a theatrical event, and direct their attention away from the actors and their art.

When an event of secondary importance is played entirely insignificantly by the actor, the event becomes annoying and even disturbing. Therefore, we may say that a certain degree of Significance must always be present, its intensity regulated by the good taste of the actor and the director. There is no place on the stage for events that are entirely insignificant. If insignificant acting reigns on the stage, the spectator begins to flounder helplessly, looking for something that can arouse his interest. In the end, he feels himself distracted and torn by the insignificance and free flow of annoying impressions. "I became so tired today during the performance," he says, "although there was nothing unusual on the stage." In just this "nothing unusual" lies the exhausting influence of insignificance.

The question may now arise as to whether the performance will not become heavy, overpowering, and cumbersome because of this constant Significance. Won't the audience be exhausted by constantly following significant events on the stage? Though theoretically it might seem that such would be the case, experience has shown that the reaction of the spectator is quite different. The more significant the impression of the piece of art, the more harmonious will be the poise and the greater satisfaction the onlooker will receive from it. Also the actor who can be significant will naturally use extreme economy in his means of expression. He will no longer need to employ the vague, feeble clichés with which he so often tries to cover psychological gaps or fill the time when he has

PORTRAITS OF MICHAEL CHEKHOV
Moscow, 1914 (top left); Paris, 1932 (top right); Riga, 1934 (lower right);
Moscow, 1924 (lower left); Ridgefield, Connecticut, 1940 (center).

Michael Chekhov co-starring with Ida Lupino and Paul Henreid in the Warner Brothers' film *In Our Time*, Hollywood, 1943.

Chekhov with Ingrid Bergman in Alfred Hitchcock's *Spellbound*, 1945.

Michael Chekhov, the Village Patriarch, with a young serf in *Song of Russia*, MGM, 1943–44.

Chekhov as the temperamental Ballet Manager in Ben Hecht's *Specter of the Rose*, Hollywood, 1945.

"The Subway," a class improvisation at the Chekhov Studio in Ridgefield, Connecticut, 1939.

"Living Statue" exercises on the lawn at Dartington Hall, England, 1937.

A Chekhov Studio Theatre production of *King Lear* with (clockwise) Hurd Hatfield (top center), Yul Brynner (top right), Beatrice Straight (bottom right), Ford Rainey (bottom center), and Mary Lou Taylor (bottom left).

Michael Chekhov illustrating his Psycho-physical Technique to Virginia and Jack Palance at Chekhov's home in California, 1952.

Michael Chekhov "orchestrating" a class at Dartington Hall in 1937.

1. Abie's father in *Abie's Irish Rose*, 1944.
2. Klestakoff in *The Inspector General*, 1921.
3. Principal character in *I Forgot*, a theatre-sketch by Anton Chekhov, 1932.
4. Malvolio in *Twelfth Night*, 1917.
5. The Drowned Man in the theatre-sketch of the same name by Anton Chekhov.
6. The title role in *Eric XIV*, 1921.
7. The title role in the play *Ivan the Terrible*, 1932.
8. The Leading Man in the German film *A Fool Through Love*, 1929–30.
9. The Ballet Manager in the film *Specter of the Rose*, 1945.
10. The Student in *Rendezvous*, an Anton Chekhov sketch, 1935.
11. Skid in *Artisten*, Vienna, 1928.
12. Leopold in the film *In Our Time*, 1943.
13. The Papa in *The Bridegroom and the Papa*, an Anton Chekhov sketch, 1931.
14. The Village Patriarch in the film *Song of Russia*, 1943–44.
15. Frazier in *Deluge*, 1915.
16. Hamlet, 1932.
17. A Gestapo agent for a proposed film, 1949.

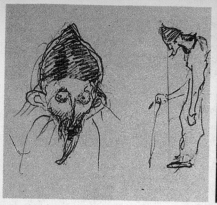

Michael Chekhov's preliminary sketches for his character Ivan the Terrible. Chekhov as Ivan, 1932, in Riga (center).

Chekhov as Senator Abeleukov.

Sketch by Michael Chekhov for Senator Abeleukov in Andrei Bely's *Petersburg*.

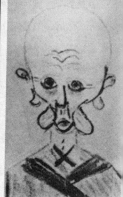

Character study sketches by Michael Chekhov for Dostoyevsky's *Selo Stepanchikovo*.

Chekhov in the role of Foma Opiskin in *Selo Stepanchikovo*.

no lines. He will always be significant without distracting, eschewing incessant, insignificant "acting" that detracts from more significant characters and scenes.

A love for the essentials of acting will soon develop in the actor, and through this, the performance will acquire a higher standard, which will guide the audience's attention along the main lines of the plot. The director will distinguish the important leading moments of the play and will smooth out places of minor importance, without making them significant! He will be able to do this much better if his actors have developed a sense of Significance in themselves.

EXERCISE 62.

Two partners improvise a scene such as the following: in a shop, the salesman and the purchaser; in a restaurant, the customer and the waiter; a host or hostess and a guest; an interviewer and a distinguished personality. While improvising, both partners must learn to recognize important moments and less significant ones. The partner who is less important at the moment must learn to diminish his Significance, giving the other partner the right to have the "lead," even if it is only for a few seconds. This exercise requires a delicate kind of execution and also long and patient work. By "giving the stage" to one's partner, one must not lose either one's own Significance or one's presence on the stage. Radiation must go on as always, but a certain kind of withdrawal, a certain veiling of the Significance must take place.

The actor who knows what Significance is can learn by experience how to increase or diminish his Significance while acting. Both partners, while trading the position of Significance, must have a feeling for the audience. Without imagining the audience attending the work, the exercises will lose part of their purpose. One must realize that diminishing the Significance does not necessarily mean that the outer action must always be lessened or stopped.

EXERCISE 63.

A group of actors takes a sketch or improvisation (the simpler the better). They choose the important leading moments to which the audience's attention must be directed. Knowing which sentence or what business, or which pause, which moment, is more important for the content of the sketch, they try to act it, pursuing the same aim as before.

The actors begin another short sketch, repeating it again and again, gradually distinguishing leading moments more and more clearly, without defining them beforehand. It may happen, of course, that one person will consider one moment important, while another will feel some other moment is more important, and the latter will try to direct the audience's attention to his chosen point. But this must not confuse the group, because it cannot be otherwise in the beginning. The more this exercise is repeated, the more the contact and sensitivity of the members of the group will unite them in finding a common desire to lead the audience's attention to one definite point. It requires time to get this inner, unspoken agreement. (In a real production, of course, the director handles the proper distribution of important moments.)

The group chooses a mob scene from a play and rehearses it, following its content. The significant moments must be determined beforehand. The part of the crowd which is not using the Significance fully in its acting at the moment should not die out. The audience must always have the impression that the whole crowd is present and active. Then the group chooses another crowd scene from a play and rehearses it as before, following its contents but without defining the leading moment beforehand.

The last variation is achieved when the mob or crowd scene is improvised by the group. Only the theme must be determined before the improvisation starts. Remember that when the actor takes part in any mob or crowd scene, he is inclined to lose his individuality and feel himself engulfed in the group of people around him—"absorbed" in it, as it were. As a consequence of such a wrong attitude, the actor begins alone to act as if he were the whole crowd. He becomes noisy and restless, and his whole behavior is "general" instead of being individual. This false and unnatural acting makes the impression that the crowd consists of dolls and puppets. An actor must elaborate his part in a crowd scene with the same care as any other individual part.

ENSEMBLE

Using all that we have said before as a basis, we now arrive at the next point in the organic structure of our method. The actor's profession is such that the actor cannot count on being alone on the stage. As a rule he is one of a group of people—an ensemble—the members of which must find the right connection with each other in order to establish a constant harmony among themselves. The more sensitive they become, through correct training, the more they depend upon each other for mutual support and inspiration. At the present time, actors do not feel so strongly the need for an ensemble, because repertory theatres have not yet found general recognition. But the time for such theatres will undoubtedly come. The very nature of scenic art requires them, and will call them forth out of an inexorable necessity. The following exercise will show a practical approach to developing ensemble technique.

<u>EXERCISE 64.</u>

The members of the group should first realize that they are together. They can do this in the following way. Using the ability of concentration, they try to keep in their minds all the participants of the exercise. They are aware of the presence of each person in the room. Then everyone has to make an inner effort to open himself to the others. This means that they are to be ready to receive the impressions—even the most delicate ones—from everyone present at that moment, and to be willing to react to them harmoniously in a friendly way, without the slightest inclination to become sentimental. One should try to avoid the feeling that one is facing a general group of people. Each person should be regarded as an individual. One must feel, not "They and I," but "He and he and she . . . and I." Through the desire of each participant to join with the others, the whole group will take the first step toward union.

When contact is established to a certain degree, the group chooses a series of actions. 1. To walk across the room slowly. 2. To run quickly. 3. To stand quietly. 4. To sit down on chairs. 5. To lie down on the floor. 6. To speak loudly together. 7. To come close together and whisper.

By opening themselves to one another, and through sensitive guessing, the group will "choose" which action it is inclined to fulfill at the moment. No previous arrangement has to be made. It may happen that the group will start by running and then will decide to sit down, or to stand quietly, and so on. This tendency to catch and realize the common desire will establish the contact among the members of the group. The "guessing" does not, of course, preclude the members of the group looking at each other. The point of the exercise is to make an effort to "guess," and in this way gradually to increase the sensitivity that is the basis for all ensemble work.

EXERCISE 65.

The actors now combine business with words. Two people, for instance, have just finished a talk. There is a pause before they separate. One of them gets up and says, "Thank you, I will think about it. Goodbye." The other catches the fine nuances in the movement, mood, and voice of his partner, and answers him, trying to be in full harmony with his previous conduct: "Goodbye. I will wait for your decision."

Let us take as an example for the whole group the beginning, or the end, of a meeting. The chairman addresses the members. He opens the debate, or concludes the meeting. How the chairman speaks, moves, listens, looks, and so on, must be the key for the acting of the participants. Here again sensitivity leads to harmonious acting by the ensemble.

EXERCISE 66.

The group chooses a theme for improvisation. Only the plot and the general order of events need be agreed upon. The improvisation will, of course, be chaotic in the beginning, but this must not discourage the participants. They must go on acting freely until, under the influence of their desire to be sensitive to each other, the improvisation becomes a well-shaped whole. The success of the exercise is not important—the effort to acquire the ability of unspoken agreement is the real aim.

A group of actors that desires to develop in the direction described above will in time acquire the happy ability of improvising every moment while acting on the stage. They will improvise freely, so that each hint given by one member while acting will be taken up by another, used, developed, and returned. We are not speaking, of course, about improvising the text or arbitrarily changing the mise-en-scène. We refer to a finer kind of improvising that can take place everywhere, at any moment during the acting. The chain of such improvised moments will not break anywhere if the actor has acquired the suggested technique, yet it will still remain completely within the framework established by the text and the director. Ensemble acting, if rightly understood, is the opposite of what we have called acting with "clichés," in which everything is outwardly fixed and inwardly deadened.

THE SENSE OF STYLE

We have already mentioned the importance in our art of differentiating the "what" (the content, the meaning) from the "how" (the manner of its Incorporation on the stage). The strongest, all-dominating "how," we might even say the supreme "how"—although the most illusive—is Style.

We must admit that in our present crude age, the actor, more than any other artist, has lost his sensitivity to style. Do we often see actors on the stage performing tragedy, drama, comedy, or vaudeville in the particular style of each of these forms? Do they take the various styles of different authors into account? Do they properly consider the different styles of the same author?

The costumes, sets, and makeup may be in a certain style, but they do not make the style of the performance if the sense of style does not live in the soul of the actor. This sense rises from the most profound depths of the human consciousness, whether in an individual or in an epoch, and cannot be imitated outwardly in stage sets and theatrical costumes.

What did humanity experience in the epoch out of which the Gothic style arose and was developed? They felt the tense conflict between earthly powers on the one hand, and a longing for light and spiritual growth on the other. The composition of a cubic form below—humanity held by the earthly world; a round form in the middle, the tendency of humanity toward quiet, introspective concentration—and the pointed form streaming upward, the prayers and feelings of humanity flying upward, were strongly experienced by man before they found their physical incorporation in the Gothic style.

How shall we compare this with the Baroque style? There, everything expresses restless, disturbed, movable human emotions. A new world outlook develops, shaking the human consciousness! A revolutionary tendency comes to the fore. Through travel, through colonization, the physical relief of the earth's surface becomes tangible for mankind. Copernicus, religious reformers, and revolutionaries change the previously quiet, dogmatic, law-abiding world conception into one of movement. Artists grasped this new world outlook and made it beautiful—the Baroque style arose.

The actor's nature undoubtedly longs for a sense of Style, as does every artistic nature. But in our time it cannot be so easily achieved without a stimulus. The modern actor should use certain exercises in his first steps toward the sense of Style. The best way to do such exercises is in a group.

EXERCISE 67.

The group chooses an abstract theme such as defeat, sorrow, revenge, victory, ecstasy, or devotion. On the basis of the chosen theme the participants build a plastic group in a certain style. For this exercise, take such different theatrical styles as tragedy, drama, comedy, vaudeville, and clown style. From different places in the room, the participants individually approach the place where the group is to be formed. While doing so they guess what kind of a group can be built from this particular theme, and in this particular style. Each approaching person seeks to adjust himself to the others and to the whole composition while it is being formed. At the end, the group will look like a piece of sculpture. The same theme must be used in connection with each style, but the groups will be different, of course, as the result of improvisation and style. Vary this exercise by taking a piece of music as the indication for the style as well as for the theme.

EXERCISE 68.

Having formed a composition in one style—tragedy, for example—the group must, without breaking the composition, change into another style—dramatic, for instance. The outward change should be as slight as possible, but the composition must, nevertheless, give the impression of another style. The same should be done with comedy, vaudeville, and clown styles. Here, as is always the case in our exercises, the inner effort to find the difference between two or more styles is the aim of the exercise. The mere physical imitation of the style will only lead the participants astray.

We have chosen the above-mentioned styles, not because they are the only possible ones, but because they are completely different and so give the actor a good opportunity to gradually awaken his own sense of style.

EXERCISE 69.

Now let the group choose a theme for an improvisation and go over it several times, following different styles, but this time having in mind different authors—as if it were a play by Shakespeare, Ibsen,

Maeterlinck, or Molière, for instance. This same improvisation can be done in the style of a folk or fairy tale, or commedia dell'arte. An even finer sense of style is needed for this exercise than for the preceding one.

EXERCISE 70.

Now imagine yourself dressed in costumes of different periods and styles. It is also desirable to imagine yourself in fantastic costumes. Imagine them as clearly as possible so that they will become a real outward expression of the inner feeling of Style. Each fold in the costume, as well as its shape and color, must be visualized and inwardly experienced. Move and speak under the inspiration of the style of the imaginary costume. Do this at first as a separate exercise, then improvise on a simple theme.

Take another theme, and in addition to the costume imagine different settings in the same style, such as Indian, Persian, Egyptian, Roman, Gothic, Renaissance, Baroque, Rococo, and so forth. In this connection also imagine fantastic styles in settings and costumes.

EXERCISE 71.

The actor can increase his sense of Style by calling up his dreams and trying to live in them as clearly as possible with his waking consciousness. Our dreams are not naturalistic or dryly intellectual. They are the products of our subconscious creation. In spite of their often chaotic character, they are nevertheless full of style. Do not pay too much attention to what your dream shows you, but rather *hów* it shows you. While remembering your dream, try to live in its Atmospheres, moods, and Feelings. Just as the fragrance of a flower is free from the plant itself, is not rooted in the earth like the plant and can be breathed even far away from the blossom, so the fragrance of dreams remains with us in our waking hours when the dreams themselves have passed away. This is what we mean by deriving a sense of Style and certain other Qualities from the "fragrance" of our dreams.

The sense of Style, when obtained from the actor's dreams, will penetrate slowly and deeply into his nature. Supported by exercises, it will even penetrate the actor's body. Steiner wrote, "The better the actor has trained himself to live with his dreams, remembering their images, putting them before his mind's eye again and again, the better posture he will have on the stage. He will acquire for himself not outer posture alone, but artistic posture, full of style." Further, he says that the actor on the stage will use his body not with skill only, but with artistic flexibility. Such flexibility can be achieved only from within, while skill can be acquired largely by means of physical training alone.

8

COMPOSITION OF THE PERFORMANCE

All art constantly aspires toward the condition of music.
WALTER PATER

PREPARATION AND SUSTAINING

Wherever we discover a true piece of art, we also find an "artistic frame." Each artistic action, however large or small, must be preceded by a preparatory activity and then followed by a sustaining moment. This creates the frame. Neither nature nor man is exempt from this law.

Here are some examples, which we must see with our artistic eye, with a little imagination and a touch of fantasy: the earth in summer is in a highly creative state. It displays all the powers it has accumulated within itself during the winter. But nature does not manifest these powers abruptly. It makes a long Preparation, which we call spring. Then, having exhausted its resources, the earth slowly withdraws its powers once again, accumulating them under its surface and preparing new seeds for the next spring. We call autumn the Sustaining.

We experience the same thing when we see a child, an animal, or a plant growing, developing, increasing in size and strength, and then, after a time, slowly wasting away, fading and withering. For the artist, dawn is the Preparation for a long summer day, with its constant fight between passion and laziness, and the twilight is a desired Sustaining.

The foundation of a Greek temple seems like the Preparation for its strong, cold, symmetric forms; and the low, triangular roof appears like the Sustaining of these forms. Now look at the Egyptian pyramid. The earth itself is its Preparation. Follow it upward and upward from the earth, and you will find its Sustaining high above its visible summit.

In observing individual pieces of art, in painting, architecture, literature, music, etc., one may find many examples, but let us turn to the theatre and discover some examples in *King Lear*. The scene preceding Lear's first appearance before the audience—we have often referred to it from other points of view—is a strongly expressed Preparation for the whole tragedy. Harmoniously corresponding with it is the Sustaining of the tragedy after Lear dies, before the last curtain falls. Inside this "frame" we find another. The accursed Cordelia, tossed away when she is speaking, and the worshiped Cordelia, hugged to the crying heart when she is silent—those are the Preparation and the Sustaining of all that lies between them.

Such "frames," large and small, can be found throughout the play. Once the actor and the director have acquired an understanding of and a love for Preparation and Sustaining in their professional work, their creations will appear significant and harmonious to the audience.

EXERCISE 72.

Execute a symmetrical gesture with your arms and hands. But just before you actually initiate the movement, try to feel the impulse for it, like a flash, as though you wish to invisibly accumulate and send out your activity for the movement before the movement commences. This is the Preparation.

Immediately after you have completed the movement, pause briefly, as though you wish to evaluate, to realize, to echo, or to let others be aware of the action that has passed. This is the Sustaining.

Vary your movements, making them more complicated and then more prolonged. The nature and duration of the Preparation and the Sustaining will depend on the significance and the duration of the action itself. Usually the Sustaining is not long—it need last for only a few seconds. (If it is longer, then it becomes a complete Pause, which we will discuss later in this chapter.) But all this must always be a matter of your taste, of your sense of artistic balance. The satisfaction you will feel in applying the technique of the Preparation and the Sustaining will be a sign that your action begins to be a well-formed, complete whole.

EXERCISE 73.

Now, instead of a movement as the basis of your exercise, take a word, then a sentence, and finally a series of sentences. The Preparation and the Sustaining are the same as before: your Activity must be sent out before the word is spoken, and afterward, the word must be allowed to fly away on the winds of your Activity.

While exercising with words, you may at first make certain movements with your arm and hand as follows: Preparation—fling out your hand (not too abruptly) as though you are making way for the word that you are going to pronounce; Sustaining—keep your hand outstretched for a while, as though you are following the word that you have sent out into the space in front of you.

Now combine the action and the word. Start with simple movements and words. End with a short improvisation with partners. Practice regularly until the use of Preparation and Sustaining becomes habitual and doesn't require your conscious attention. You cannot improvise, rehearse, or act while consciously thinking of the exercises. They must frame and perfect your acting without your conscious participation. Through correct Preparation and Sustaining, you will realize more and more that all we call art comes always from an impulse from inside. Furthermore, this realization will be a good guarantee against clichés, which come from outside and remain on the surface, covering and imprisoning all the true creative impulses of an artist.

COMPOSITION AS AN ARTISTIC FRAME

But, one might ask, how can the audience know about all these frames? How can the actor express them on the stage? Is it not an intellectual game on the part of the actor and the director, which the onlooker will never become aware of? Such a question, however, would be just and correct if it were amplified to apply to all the principles of the Composition. How will the audience know, for instance, that the play has been divided into three main parts, each one with its polarity, similarity, climaxes, accents, metamorphosis, Rhythmical Waves, and Repetitions?

This question requires a thorough answer, but let us first

agree that there is an insurmountable barrier between understanding and experience, knowledge and ability. The difference is not only a quantitative one. As the experience penetrates into the very heart of the problem, whereas understanding remains on the surface of it, we naturally may expect the right answer to our question only if it comes from experience itself, and the experience is the following:

As soon as the actor absorbs the network of the Composition of the play, he begins to feel, while rehearsing or acting, that all scenes or moments in the play are present at each moment. For him time loses its usual meaning. Regardless of their succession in time he senses them all with equal acuteness. For him the succession of events becomes but an outer necessity that he has to reckon with if he wishes to convey his creative conception to others, while this conception itself is ever present in him. The natural function of the creative human spirit is to unite and to synthesize, contrary to the intellect, which divides and analyzes. A sense of Composition serves such unification.

If the actor appearing as King Lear amid the splendor of the throne room, surrounded by his children and courtiers, is not burning with the desire to die as a lonely, homeless beggar on the battlefield—he is not yet in possession of his part. And when dying on the battlefield, if he is not stunned by the vision of his majestic entrance in the beginning—he does not yet know the "magic" of the theatre. But as soon as he is changed, the miracle happens of itself. The past and the future, being experienced acutely as the present, are mighty means for completely changing the actor himself. All that he bears within himself, with love and trepidation, flies powerfully across the footlights to the audience. Even in our everyday life, where we do nothing but hide ourselves from others, we still can "feel" the person whom we meet.

When the actor truly and acutely experiences all the principles of Composition we have spoken about, they transform themselves into his heart and Will. But if the actor manages to make his heart mute and his Will flabby, the audience surely will not be enchanted by the harmony of the composition! Or even worse, it will "see" all the divisions and subdivisions, all the accents, contrasts, Transitions and repetitions. It will see the bare scheme of the production. Woe then to the director, the actor, the author, and the whole performance itself!

Another factor that will enable the audience to experience the Composition of the performance is provided by the laws of Composition themselves. They extend their numerous threads from each point of the play to all the others, binding and holding them together. Following threads, the audience will inevitably follow the Composition itself, experiencing it as a complete whole, just as the actors do on the stage while performing.

COMPOSITIONARY GESTURE

The actor cannot comprehend Composition and Rhythm if they are not experienced and felt inwardly. The internal experience is beyond any verbal, intellectual explanation. An exercise properly done can tell the actor more than pages and pages in books on Composition and Rhythm. The exercises in this chapter will enable the actor to apply the laws of Composition with ease, truthfulness, and great artistic satisfaction. Their aim is to create in the actor's psychology that harmonious form which we call the Compositionary Gesture.

EXERCISE 74.

Start with simple, wide movements. Shape them well. Use the whole space you have at your disposal, walking, running, or jumping in it. You may even use steps or platforms. Each time consciously frame your movement with the idea of Preparation and Sustaining in mind. Repeat each movement until you are able to perform it easily.

Apart from the points of Preparation and Sustaining, realize the beginning and the end of the movement. Feel the polarity of the beginning and end, and make it clearer in the movement itself. Then experience the middle part as a metamorphosis between the two poles.

Shape a climactic moment in each of the three parts. This means to find an additional short movement, or second climax, in the middle section as well as in the beginning and end. Make the second moment inwardly more tense than the general movement itself.

Determine which Qualities you can do for your movement in the beginning and the end. See that the first and the last climaxes are also polar, and that the middle part and its climax make a real Transition from one pole to the next.

Having elaborated and improved your movement, rehearse it until it becomes a beautiful miniature piece of art. Don't go from one stage of the exercise to the next before you are entirely free and satisfied with the previous one.

EXERCISE 75.

Add words to the three-part movement. For each part choose a word or a sentence that matches the Qualities you have chosen for the movement. You may also use lines of verse with their corresponding Qualities.

Continue this exercise until you need think neither of Preparation and Sustaining, nor of the three parts, the polarities, and climaxes. The initial effort must be replaced by the pleasure of carrying out the exercise. Now invent other movements and develop them in the same way. (While working on other exercises, occasionally return to this one.)

EXERCISE 76.

Take any naturalistic theme from your imagination or a literary source. From it, create a short sketch or improvisation, which may include other actors. As far as possible, uncover its composition as imaginatively and intuitively as you can, i.e., agree with your partners upon the three main parts, the three climaxes, the polarity, and main Qualities. Start to improvise once or twice. Then see what positive and negative results come from your efforts. Agree upon the corrections. Improvise again. Make new corrections. Do this until you are satisfied.

Find subdivisions, auxiliary climaxes, and accents. Do not think them out forcibly, but follow your imagination and artistic intuition. Improvise again until you feel that through corrections and repeated improvising you have become familiar with the sketch and are able to act it easily, fulfilling your Composition.

Now try to forget the content and try to revive in your mind only the Compositionary Gesture you have created and followed in your sketch. Listen to it as to "music." Return again to the sketch.

EXERCISE 77.

Concentrate your attention upon Rhythmical Waves and Repetitions. Work out a wide, threefold movement as before, without climaxes and words. Rehearse it with polarities and Qualities, with Preparation and Sustaining movements. In each part include one wavelike variation—a slight holding back, a slight quickening, slight variation of the movement itself, increased or decreased intensity, expansion, or concentration. Add more and more waves throughout the entire movement. Make them similar, so that they can represent for you the waves as well as the Repetitions. For a while, keep this exercise separate from the previous ones, but when you feel secure in all of them, merge them.

PAUSE

We know that on the stage, acting must take place all the time, uninterruptedly. But it can assume two different forms; one expresses itself outwardly, the other inwardly. The strongest inner activity is a complete Pause. The Pause as emptiness, as a full stop, does not exist on the stage. The main characteristic of a true Pause is a moment of absolute Radiation.

Between a complete Pause and fully expressed outer acting, when the Pause disappears entirely, are innumerable degrees and variations. From the point of view of Composition and Rhythm, where everything becomes a kind of "music," where everything moves, fluctuates, interweaves, we always experience a Pause on the stage. The Pause disappears only in those cases when the outer action is complete, when everything becomes outwardly expressed. Therefore, we may say that the stronger the outer action on the stage, the more incomplete is the Pause, and vice versa.

We find many good examples of incomplete Pauses in *King Lear.* In the very beginning of the play, when Gloucester and Kent have their dialogue, the whole scene has the character of an incomplete Pause. We expect Lear's appearance, we feel that the main action has not yet begun, that it remains inward. The Atmosphere of expectation fills the stage with strong Radiation. All of this makes us feel that, simultaneously with the action, there is also a Pause on the stage that gives great inner significance to the scene regardless of the words that are spoken.

We find another such example at the end of the scene in *Lear* when the two sisters plot against their father. Other examples of incomplete Pauses, which gradually become complete ones, are found in the scenes where Lear falls into a deathlike sleep on the heath and at the very end of the play, when he dies.

How the complete Pause is transformed into complete outer action, and therefore disappears entirely, can be shown in the scene in which, after Cordelia's words "Nothing, my lord," a complete Pause emerges and then, little by little, gives way to the outer action of Lear's passionate fury.

There are two kinds of Pauses, one of which appears before a certain event takes place. It foretells what is to come. On the stage it awakens the audience's anticipation. Through it the onlooker is prepared to receive the approaching scene. He is spellbound by it. Such a Pause, for instance, is the one before Lear's first entrance in the throne room. The other kind of Pause, quite opposite in character, appears after the action is fulfilled, and is a summing up of all that has happened before. In the last act, after Lear's death, the Pause summarizes the psychological result of the previous happenings.

Numerous examples of Pauses can be found in every play. The Pause as the expression of the inner life always dominates a greater part of plays than we are accustomed to think. Having thus broadened our conception of the Pause, we naturally shall enrich our means of expression, thus making the performance more significant, more inward, alive and also well shaped from the point of view of the Composition.

PAUSE AND ATMOSPHERE

The Pause has an affinity to Atmosphere. Both are inward, must strongly radiate from the performer, and are rooted in the realm of the feelings. Actors know from their own experience that if they succeed in creating a good, significant Pause on the stage, the Atmosphere emerges immediately and fascinates the audience. Conversely, if there is a strong Atmosphere on the stage, the actor instinctively uses every opportunity to "hold a Pause," which will strengthen the atmosphere and so attract the audience's attention.

EXERCISE 78.

Start an improvisation with a long Pause that has resulted from a previous scene. This could be a meeting scene, a philosophical conversation, a wild party, or a rest period after some physically exhausting activity. Establish the Atmosphere in terms of the original situation and experience the Pause as the result of the action that preceded it.

During this first Pause, gradually transform it into a second Pause out of which a new scene will emerge. If the exercise is done by a group, see that a strong ensemble feeling unites all the participants. When the group feels that the Pause is "ripe" enough to give birth to a new scene, continue the improvisation with words and business in keeping with the chosen theme.

The scene must resolve itself at the end into still another Pause, which will be a sum of all the previous acting. Hold the Pause and after a while again transform it, as before, into one from which you can continue the improvisation. Repeat the alternating rhythms of external and inner acting and the transformation of the Pauses.

Create any Atmosphere and experience it as a Pause. Realize how both Atmosphere and Pause strengthen each other. Perform some short action with words in this Atmosphere, and then again hold the Pause. Be sure that the Atmospheres and the Radiation do not weaken during the Pause. Return to previous exercises, inserting in them different kinds of Pauses.

EXERCISE 79.

Read a play, stopping at places where you think a complete Pause might occur. Experience it inwardly. Compare different Pauses, evaluating their individual characteristics. Go over the play, looking for incomplete Pauses. Try to experience the degree of their incompleteness and their general character.

CRESCENDO AND DIMINUENDO

The complete Pause, on the one hand, and the complete outer action on the other, are two poles between which the Diminuendo and the Crescendo swing. But also within a complete Pause the actors—and consequently the audience, too—can experience Crescendo as well as Diminuendo. Actors who develop the ability to control these two principles in all their subtleties discover psychological nuances in their own acting that they did not even know they possessed.

EXERCISE 80.

Experience shows that the most difficult form of Crescendo and Diminuendo is the one that rises and falls slowly, evenly, and smoothly. Begin this exercise alone. Develop out of the Pause any simple business, lead it to the extreme outer form of action, and then return to the Pause. All this must be done without any jumps, leaps, or jerking.

Do the exercise in a group. See that a strong ensemble feeling is established. Do the exercise in the form of an improvisation. Avoid complicated themes and business at first. See that all your words, voices, movements, mise-en-scène, even the objects you use while improvising, such as chairs, tables, and properties, fulfill a smooth, even Crescendo and Diminuendo. Do this several times to be sure that you can justify everything you do and thus make your acting truthful and natural.

EXERCISE 81.

Start to exercise variations of Crescendo and Diminuendo. Do not discuss the form of the variation you are going to work on, but "agree" by drawing a curve, if possible on the blackboard, and then try to fulfill it. Such an "agreement" will awaken a finer sensitivity among the members of the group than will the usual manner of discussion. After doing the exercise, each of the participants draws on the blackboard his impression as to how it was done. At first the "opinions" expressed on the blackboard will differ, but after a certain period of exercising the sensitivity of the group will grow, and a correct fulfillment as well as correct judgment will gradually develop. Pass from one variation to another, making only slight alterations at first.

Take a short scene from a play and rehearse it for one aim only, which will be to fulfill the pattern of Crescendo and Diminuendo agreed upon. (If necessary, discuss it, but finally draw it on the blackboard in the form of a curve, as suggested above.) After you succeed with this scene, take some simple characterization for each part. Try to fulfill the same pattern of Crescendo and Diminuendo as before.

EXERCISE 82.

Rehearse a scene or do an improvisation without defining any pattern beforehand. After the exercise is completed, each member of the group should draw his conception of how it should have been done. Take into consideration all the curves that have been drawn, and without discussing them repeat the scene.

Draw your suggestions again for the next run-through, and rehearse again, until the whole group has arrived at an opinion that will be satisfactory to everyone. Each member should try to be as flexible as possible in accepting the suggestions of the others.

TEMPO

Our usual conception of Tempo on the stage does not distinguish its two different aspects, the inner and the outer. The first can be defined as a person's quick or slow change and Transformation in the mind, Feelings, and Will-impulses. The second expresses itself in a person's quick or slow outer behavior.

These types of Tempo are so different that they can be observed simultaneously, even in cases where they are completely contradictory. A person is waiting impatiently for something. Picture after picture may flash through his mind. His Feelings and Will are aroused and stirred, changing with lightning speed, and yet he can control himself to such an extent that all his movements, his speech, and his outer behavior will be completely opposite to his feverish inner state. The outer Tempo will be slow while the inner will be extremely quick. The opposite can be observed when, for instance, skillful, habitual work is being done in a quick outer Tempo, while the inner life of the person runs simultaneously in a quiet, slow Tempo. When these two kinds of Tempo are kept apart and used on the stage simultaneously, they always produce a strong impression upon the audience. Here again the law of contrasts in art shows its fascinating power.

A slow inner or outer Tempo should not, however, be confused with passivity on the stage. The actor has to be always active, always present and awake on the stage, whatever Tempo he uses in his acting. On the other hand, a quick Tempo must not be mistaken for physical, muscular tension. Quick Tempo must also be distinguished from simple haste, a distinction rarely made on the stage. Haste usually makes a different impression on the audience than the one the actor hopes to create.

To avoid these mistakes, the actor should keep the following suggestions in mind. First, maintaining a sense of the character's Objective will help the actor to kill haste and unnecessary tension, on the one hand, and will protect him from passivity on the other hand. Second, a flexible and obedient body together with a fine technique of speech obtained through training will help the quick Tempo. No difficulties must arise from the technical side. Third, the actor can find help in establishing the true Tempo by imagining the air around him as moving and vibrating in the proper Tempo. This image will be especially useful during the first period of rehearsing.

Different Tempos change the Qualities and even the meaning of an action. A simple example can explain this. Say "Good-bye" or "How do you do?" in different Tempos, and you will see how the Qualities of these words and even the meaning of the departure or the meeting will change with the Tempo. Any action, however complicated it may be, changes under the influence of Tempo. This means that the actor can use Tempo not only as a means of shaping a Compositionary pattern but also as a means of awakening and enriching his Feelings and his inner life on the stage.

Misuse of the Tempo, as of the Pause, can have harmful effects, however. Accidental change of Tempo or acting throughout the whole play in the same Tempo obscures the meaning and makes the performance dull. The ability to use the right Tempo at the right place must become a subconscious skill on the part of the actor. Tempo, which plays a most important part in Crescendo and Diminuendo in the method, has to be exercised separately.

EXERCISE 83.

Carry out any business, alone or in a group, keeping the same Tempo. Repeat, using different Tempos. Now perform a simple improvisation, changing the Tempo within it. Draw different curves of this exercise on the blackboard, as shown before. Avoid any complicated task until you are able to perform the simple ones.

EXERCISE 84.

Create an improvisation, preferably with a group, distinguishing between the outer and inner Tempos. For example, choose a scene in an operating room involving the surgeon, his assistants, and nurses. A dangerous operation is taking place. To save the life of the patient the operation must be accomplished as quickly as possible. Tension. The inner Tempo is extremely fast. All movements and short cues, on the contrary, are cautious, controlled and reserved. The outer Tempo is slow.

Here is another improvisation. Servants of a big, wealthy family are packing numerous suitcases and trunks. The family is going on a journey. The butler, supervising the work of the servants, hurries them. The packing goes on quickly and skillfully. The outer Tempo is fast. But the servants, indifferent to the family's excitement, are inwardly calm and placid, knowing that there is plenty of time. Here the inner Tempo is slow.

Now make both Tempos fast. In a small town, preparations for a local festival are being made. The crowd in the street decorates the houses. Both the inner and outer Tempos are quick.

Now let us make both Tempos slow. A group, after a long and tiring picnic, is about to move homeward. People lazily gather their belongings, bid farewell to each other, and enter their automobiles. Both Tempos are slow. Don't confuse the laziness of the characters with inactivity on the actor's part.

EXERCISE 85.

Use the same theme several times for different variations of Tempo, since this will give you a sharper experience of the Tempo itself, regardless of the theme. One part of the group acts in one Tempo, the other in another. For example, the servants are packing suitcases in a slow inner Tempo but a quick outer Tempo, in the presence of members of the family, who are in a state of quick inner Tempo but slow, controlled outer Tempo. Form any combinations of Tempo you choose.

EXERCISE 86.

Exercise the Tempo as a stimulus for changing the Qualities of the acting. Do the same short improvisation repeatedly in different Tempos, giving attention exclusively to the changes that come to you while you are improvising. Choose the Tempo without thinking or suggesting in advance what psychological nuances it may call up in you. However, having chosen the Tempo let it influence you while you are improvising. See that you are truthful in each psychological variation that arises.

EXERCISE 87.

Read any play and try to visualize the scene you have chosen in different Tempos. Find out which Tempo is the right one and which will satisfy your artistic taste to the fullest extent. See also how this scene's Qualities and perhaps the meaning alter under the influence of the different Tempos.

9

FOUR STAGES
OF THE
CREATIVE
PROCESS

The more the marble wastes,
the more the statue grows.
MICHELANGELO

Let us regard the whole creative process in theatre as consist-
ing of four successive stages. Knowledge of these will give the
actor assurance in his work and will free him from the slavery
of accidents, personal moods, disappointments, and nervous
impatience. These are the enemies of the actor who is unaware of the sound way of creating a part.

Let us imagine that a group of actors has become interested
in the practical elaboration of the method we have suggested,
and that they begin working on a play. This being an ideal
situation, their director too embraces the various techniques
described in this book. We shall follow their work in general

outline through the various stages, and at the same time we shall have the opportunity of flying over the whole method and surveying it.

FIRST STAGE

The first stage is the most intimate and subtle, in which the conception of the whole future performance and all the characters takes place. All is anticipation, expectation, and hopeful guessing. The actors have received their parts. Whether the parts are new or well known to them does not in the least affect that typical joy that arises in their hearts, signifying that the work has begun.

The Higher Ego experiences the flutterings of "first love." Eagerness to meet the future audience; confidence in it and in oneself; the hope of being able to express dear, intimate things in one's own way, individually and freely—all this is the actor's experience at this moment. Deep in the hidden regions of his soul, where the Creative Individuality is always active, the preparatory work goes on and must not be disturbed too early by conscious interference. The general, all-embracing Atmosphere is, for the actor, a first sign of the work that his subconscious mind is now performing on the whole play.

First, the actors must be fed by the idea, the general Atmosphere, the style, the dynamic of good and evil, and the social significance of the play. At this period of the work, the characters become an organic part of the whole, and so they remain during all the following stages, if their hidden development has not been disturbed in the beginning. At a later time, the actor accumulates the potential ability to express the entire play, at each moment and in every detail.

This initial work springs from the ever active and artistically wise Higher Ego. The more conscientious the work of the actors in assuming the suggested method has been, the more successful will be the subconscious process. This early stage, if rightly understood and carried out, is a guarantee against over- or underemphasis of a single character. Conversely, prematurely isolating a character from the whole composition of the play at this time may cause many difficulties for the actor later on and may even turn newly born characters into artistic perversions.

Living in the general Atmosphere of the play, the actors should read the whole play for themselves again and again, observing the images arising out of this Atmosphere. The images of this period are usually very ephemeral and transitory, but they all reveal to the actors new, exciting, and promising ideas. Here the actor can really learn what it is to be able to wait actively!

As they enjoy the interplay of images, the actors may feel gradually attracted to some more than to others; they should try not to interfere with the subtle process of inner formation and choice. Their concern is still the same—to see the images as clearly as possible in spite of their mobility and great independence.

Actors will find it both exciting and useful to start at this stage a kind of "diary," in which they make notes of their visions in a few sketchy words, simple drawings, and even in a few free lines, using perhaps colored pencils. Such a "diary" will remind the actors of their first fluctuating and ephemeral images, which without such a "diary" could easily be forgotten and therefore lost for the future work. Going over these notes in later stages of the work, actors will also find that images, ideas, and creative impulses have developed of themselves, and from the pages of their "diaries" actors will get new, exciting inspirations. Impressions of certain dreams recorded in the diary can often be useful as well.

After a time the actors will be urged to concentrate more and more on their own characters, which at moments will demand certain intervention on the part of the actor. This does not mean that the image wants to give up its independence. On the contrary, it will increase its own activity, having been stimulated by the actor's conscious interference. At this point, Leading Questions are the right technical means to be used.

The Higher Ego sends out more and more images, which are the messengers of its marvelous activity. They descend into the realm of the conscious life of the actor, and this is a sign that the second stage must begin, in which the actors start to work methodically on their images. The first stage resembles listening to a distant musical melody with its rhythms, interwoven themes, and audible images, and does not need to be stopped abruptly when the second stage begins. The two can continue simultaneously for a long time.

SECOND STAGE

Conscious elaboration of the images, the questioning "creative gaze," and an active search for better and more expressive images characterize the second stage. The main part of the work still lies in the sphere of the imagination. Even rehearsals with partners and director constitute "imagining" the play, the situations and the characters, under the guidance of the director. He puts Leading Questions before the actors, combining them so that they make his idea, his interpretation of the play, the style, and the nature of the future performance clearer and clearer to the actors.

The director will do well to give his first Leading Questions a broad and general character. Of course, the director must have formed the main conception of the performance before he calls the cast together for the first rehearsal. He may ask the actors to see the main situations of the play one after the other in their imagination, he may lead the actors through the score of Atmospheres, ask questions about the social meaning of theatre, give hints and indications for characterizations, and stir the actors' imaginations by picturesque descriptions, by sketches of costumes and sets.

The actors fulfill the director's suggestions, and the imaginary performance grows. The director's Leading Questions have laid the foundation for the united work of all the participants. The director makes notes of his questions and of how far he has led his actors, which gives him a clear picture of the state of the yet invisible performance. He carefully prepares his questions for each rehearsal. Without discussions, theorizing, or killing analysis, the work goes on quickly, and the understanding between the director and the actors becomes stronger.

At the second stage the director also uses the principle of the Psychological Gestures. He shows them to the actors, applying them to larger or smaller sections of the text, to climactic moments, and to probable characterizations. He also asks the actors to show him their Psychological Gestures and takes them under consideration as signs of what the actors' individual interpretations might be. Although the principle of Incorporation belongs to the next stage, the actors may, while using the Psychological Gesture, now try to move and speak on the basis of it.

The director should also as much as possible describe to his cast his vision of the future performance in the form of word pictures. The actors must listen to such descriptions, imagining all that they hear.

Each actor must memorize the text as soon as possible so that the work later on will not be disturbed by efforts to remember the lines. If, during memorization, some visions of the future performance come to the actor he should enjoy them and appreciate their value in his work.

The cast begins reading the play. Each member reads his part aloud, imagining simultaneously his probable acting and that of the others. The director may ask his actors when imagining during the rehearsals and at home to do so in different ways. For instance, they may take the same scene first from the point of view of Ease, then Form, then Beauty, then Atmosphere, then Style, and then Characterization. Such reading will naturally take more time than under ordinary circumstances when only the words are pronounced. Readings may be repeated many times.

THIRD STAGE

Soon such material and activity will be accumulated in the actor's imagination, and the next step will become a pleasant necessity. Now the real work of Incorporation begins. This will be the third and longest stage. The first stage, the "musical" one, has transformed itself into the second, the "imaginary" period. The third stage is that of giving real visible and audible existence to the images. The Incorporation of characters and moments from the play is now the main occupation of all the participants.

The third stage does not start suddenly, nor does the second stage stop at once. The four stages overlap and by no means have to be understood or used in a precise, pedantic way. The rehearsals can at any time take any course that may be required to further the work. All that is required is a general adherence to the succession of the four stages.

The best way to proceed with the work in the third stage is to create a series of Incorporations of the characters with short moments from the play. The director may ask his actors such questions as the following: What do the arms, the hands, the shoulders, the feet of your character look like at such and such moments? How does the character walk, sit, or run in other moments? How does it enter, exit, listen, look? How does it react to different impressions received from other characters? How does it behave when enveloped in a certain Atmosphere?

In answer to the director's questions, the actors incorporate their visions before him. For his part, the director also incorporates his visions before his actors, making his corrections and suggestions in this way. The performers, having received the director's advice, incorporate their visions again and again before him, improving them with each new demonstration. So begins the "conversation" between the director and the cast concerning the characters and the play.

Soon such visible and audible moments accumulate in great numbers. Of course, the actors can use the text while incorporating, even before they have begun their concentrated work on it. The director will make the whole work more sensible if, before the rehearsals begin, he prepares a list of things he wants his actors to incorporate. He should have in mind that the order and the nature of his questions must help the cast to embrace the play in its entirety as well as assist the individual performer to encompass his own part as a whole, long before he is able to act it uninterruptedly from beginning to end.

During this work, the actor can create images for certain words in the text that he considers important. The actor must develop and elaborate these images so strongly that when he pronounces the words from the stage, the strength of the images behind them and all the Feelings and Will-impulses aroused by them will be "heard" in and through these words. While perfecting such images, the actor must try to create them so that they will express more the character's state of mind than his own. Try, for instance, to follow all the instances when King Lear pronounces the words "daughter," "daughters," "children," "Regan," "Goneril," and "Cordelia," and you will see what different images arise in his mind each time. The actor must develop and cherish these images of Lear's mind; then they will merge of themselves with the actor's words, making them alive, strong, and meaningful and expressive when he pronounces them from the stage.

The actors may accompany their words with movement if they wish. Here, too, the director must conduct the actor's individual work so that it will become a harmonious part in the growth of the performance. It would be wrong to concentrate too early on one scene only, leaving the rest of the play untouched for a long period of time. The performance will ripen more organically if the cast is given the opportunity to fly over the whole play at each stage of the work and even, if possible, during rehearsals. Later on, when detailed and careful work on certain scenes is needed, it will not be so easy to do this.

Such separate but leading and significant moments will serve the actors as "signposts," indicating their general approach to the play. The surer the cast is in these selected moments of both acting, through Incorporation and the Psychological Gesture, and speech, the easier will be the approach to the rest of the play. The performers and director must find a series of Psychological Gestures that will fill the gaps between selected moments in a short, concise form. The gaps will become smaller, and soon the director will find his actors ready and prepared enough to rehearse series of scenes, entire acts, and even the whole play without interruption.

What are the benefits of such an approach? First, it does not require the actor to act or speak more than he is able at the moment. He is free from the burden of having to act at any cost, hiding his lack of preparation behind a variety of clichés. Second, the short, easily comprehensible version helps the actors to continuously experience the whole play and the performance and not be distracted or fragmented by many details.

Further on, the rehearsals take a different course. The director chooses certain "grounds" for rehearsing, as, for instance, the Atmosphere of a scene or an act. The cast, while rehearsing in this way, pays attention only to the Atmosphere. The actors try to maintain the Atmosphere with all that they do or speak on the stage. They must rely upon it and must try to be fully influenced and inspired by it.

Now the director changes the rehearsal work on Atmosphere to exercises related to the Feeling of Ease, Form, Style, Activity, Psychological Gesture, Ensemble, Significance, or Radiation. The director may keep the same "ground" for several rehearsals if he finds that it has not yet been mastered, or he may return to the previous "grounds." Later, two, three, and even more "grounds" can be combined.

Qualities represent a very useful technical means of rehearsing. They can be used with the Psychological Gesture or without it. Qualities can be applied directly to the acting, and they will call up the feelings of the actor just as they do in connection with the Psychological Gesture. When rehearsing with certain "grounds," all the text and full acting can be used.

From time to time the actors should have a partial or complete run-through, acting absolutely freely, without any "grounds" or other conditions. The director makes his notes, and then rehearses with the actors those moments and places he wishes to improve. It is always better to rehearse all the corrections immediately so that the actors will not forget or misunderstand them. Special attention must be paid to the work on Characterizations in which the Imaginary Body and the Imaginary Center are used. As soon as the actors have assumed their characterizations to a certain degree, this can also be taken as a "ground" for rehearsing.

The work naturally moves from general conceptions to more detailed ones. At this stage the director interferes more often with details of acting for his cast. The best way for the director to do this is to show his actors what he wants them to do by acting before them all. The actors, if they are trained according to the suggested method, will easily understand what the director shows them, and will grasp its essence. They will not need to copy their director outwardly, as might be the case with purely external actors.

As soon as the director starts rehearsals of bits and scenes, he also begins to establish the mise-en-scène. Here his concern must be that each movement, change of place, and position of the actor on the stage will be an artistic necessity and will serve the expressiveness of the moment or the character. The actor should not be satisfied by a simply "natural" mise-en-scène without special meaning and significance.

During the period in which the makeup, costumes, sets,

and lighting are added to the production, the actors very often lose some of their previous achievements. Two things can help to diminish possible disharmony at this point. First, one or two rehearsals should be set aside especially for adjusting the actors to the costumes, makeup, and sets without too much concern being given to the standard of acting. Second, after these difficulties are more or less removed, a few rehearsals (with makeup and costumes) must be allowed for the actors to regain all lost qualities, details, and nuances of acting. Only then should so-called dress rehearsals be started.

FOURTH STAGE

The fourth stage of the creative process comes naturally as a result of the three previous ones. Using our method, the actor puts aside physical and psychological obstacles in his nature, thus freeing his creative powers. The actor should never worry about his talent, but rather about his lack of technique, his lack of training, and his lack of understanding of the creative process. The talent will flourish immediately of itself as soon as the actor chisels away all the extraneous matter that hides his abilities—even from himself.

The fourth stage involves the actor's inspiration. Everything changes for him at this happy moment. As the creator of his character, he becomes inwardly free of his own creation and becomes the observer of his own work. The actor acquires a Divided Consciousness. He has given to his image his flesh and blood, his ability to move and speak, to feel, to wish, and now the image disappears from his mind's eye and exists within him and acts upon his means of expression from inside him. This is the aim of the whole creative process, the true desire of the Higher Ego of the actor. The consciousness now stands divided.

"The actor must not be possessed by his role," wrote Rudolf Steiner. "He must stand facing it so that his part becomes objective. He experiences it as his own creation. With his ego, he stands beside his creation and is still able to enjoy its extreme joys and sorrows, as if he were facing the outer world."

Of course, there are numerous individual ways of experiencing this state of Inspiration. Steiner quoted a famous Austrian performer as stating, "I would certainly not be able to do any acting at all if I relied, on the stage, upon myself as I am—a little hunchback with a scraping voice and hideous face. As this person I couldn't do anything, of course. But here I have helped myself." And he goes on to describe his Divided Consciousness, in which his "real, ideal and entirely spiritual being" acts upon the scraping-voiced hunchback.

Another example, connected with the private life of Goethe, was related by Dr. Steiner. "Goethe's connections with this or that woman he loved were such that the most beautiful lyric reactions arose from them. How was this possible? It was possible because Goethe was constantly in a certain kind of divided consciousness of his being. While he experienced outwardly even in the most intimate moments which were very close to his heart, Goethe was always in such a division of his personality. He was Goethe whose love was not weaker than that of anyone else, but at the same time he was Goethe who observed. Goethe could always draw back, out and from himself, feeling and contemplating his own experience."

Understanding how the impulse of Creative Individuality streams through each of the four stages enables the actor to manage this process of dividing himself from his character. Although the inspiration, and with it the Divided Consciousness, come of themselves, the actor must, nevertheless, develop the habit of seeing himself objectively as an outsider. He can peek at himself in his private life, observing how he walks, how he speaks, what gestures he makes, which characteristic physical features he uses in his everyday life, and so on. He must also listen objectively to his voice. Patient and quiet exercise will lead the actor to experience one part of his being—his body and voice—as an instrument belonging to himself. He will gradually experience the other part of his being as an artistic ego, as his Creative Individuality, as the possessor of the instrument.

The actor with a Divided Consciousness will be far from those who say, "All is forgotten around me when I act," or "The audience does not exist for me," or "On the stage I have the same real feelings as in life." This attitude numbs the actor's consciousness. I know that many individuals have adopted this point of view for their work on the stage, yet I believe that this can only be the sign of limited talent and also may lead to hysterics in the actor's private life. The Higher Ego—the real artist in us—does not take part in this kind of acting! This second type of actor frequently asks, "How can I love my child if I have never had one?" "How can I die with Juliet if I have never died before?" He does not know that if he created from his Higher Ego, he would never need to repeat his personal life experience on the stage. He would never try to be on the stage "as he is in life," because this would seem tasteless to him.

Such a performer does not know that he has to invent, to create anew in his Imagination actions like death, murder, and love. If he knew this, he would be able to appreciate the older Goethe's remarks on what he had written as a young man of twenty-two. Goethe was astonished by the truthfulness of his earlier writing, and said, "I had not, of course, experienced and seen such things, but I undoubtedly had the knowledge of many varied human states through the ability of anticipation." Goethe had a similar opinion of Byron and wrote that for Byron the whole world was transparent, and his creativity was possible through anticipation. But such anticipation or creating anew is possible for the actor only if he has found the way to free his Higher Ego and to experience the Divided Consciousness.

The first sparks of inspiration may come at any moment in any stage of the work. If they come they must be welcomed and no conscious application of the method should interfere with such moments.

First Stage: Anticipation, General Atmosphere, Musical perception of the whole, first flashes of Images. Many solitary readings of the play.

Second Stage: Conscious elaboration of Images. Ensemble reading of the play. Director's Leading Questions.

Third Stage: Incorporation.

Fourth Stage: Inspiration. Divided Consciousness.

WITH
MICHAEL CHEKHOV
IN HOLLYWOOD:

For the Motion Picture and Television Actor

By MALA POWERS

During the last ten years of his life, Michael Chekhov worked in Hollywood as both actor and teacher. He deplored the fact that the television and motion picture actor often has insufficient time to prepare his or her role. Frequently the actor must both memorize and prepare the part literally overnight. The wonderful freedom and joy that comes from experimenting with a character, from ensemble playing, from discovering nuances, is in most cases denied to the modern film actor. Yet Chekhov knew that even under such adverse circumstances, the actor's inner resources can be put to use. He sought for and found ways to help the actor who is given little time to prepare a role to reduce his sense of frustration and rely on his own talent to bring true creativity and originality instead of mere clichés. Chekhov taught that with sufficient practice and exercise of the basic Technique plus some inventive and simple shortcuts to preparing the part, the actor's talent can effortlessly accommodate the hurry-up demands of film and TV work. He can become a totally expressive, instantly responsive professional actor.

WORKING WITH CHEKHOV

During many of my private sessions with Michael Chekhov he taught me his Technique of acting by actually working on the motion picture or television script in which I was about to perform. He never read my scripts. He would say to me, "Now, tell me about the script." And I would describe my character and tell him the plot of the screenplay. I wasn't aware until much later that as I quite simply and spontaneously described my character and the story, I was showing him exactly how I was going to portray the part. Later still, I realized that an artist's creative imagination immediately goes into high gear when he or she describes the play and the character before having a chance to "think" about it, before forming intellectual preconceptions.

FINDING THE CHARACTER

Chekhov would then begin to ask questions; the first was always "Is this predominantly a 'Thinking' character, a 'Feeling' character, or a 'Will' character?" Chekhov maintained that few characters, indeed, few people in real life, are evenly balanced in regard to their "Thinking," "Feeling," and "Will" forces. When acting, it is quite valuable to know whether you are working with a character who has strong Will forces and relatively little intellectual power or one who has a strong Feeling life but little ability to take hold of his Will forces.

Chekhov would further inquire, "What kind of Thinking does your character have?" Thinking can be cold and hard, like a little black rubber ball, or quick and brilliant, traveling in flashes. It can be fuzzy, light, slow and ponderous, sharp, jagged, penetrating—the types and qualities of Thinking are almost unlimited.

The same holds true for Feelings. "What kind of Feeling does your character possess?" The character can have a Feeling life that is intense and passionate, lukewarm and lugubrious, or basically bitter like a lemon. The character can have predominantly heavy Feelings that drag it down, or light, sun-filled Feelings that easily radiate to all other characters. The variety is endless.

There are all kinds of "Will" as well—despotic, cold and steely, fiery, sporadic, and so on. Although Thinking and Feeling are easily grasped, many students do not easily understand or experience what "Will" really is. They often try to understand it from the standpoint of "willpower," but Chekhov taught us to get in touch with "Will" by having us Will something to happen or by asking us to project or radiate Will. Gradually he led us to enter the realm of the Will. After a time, "Will" became a clear experience.

Mischa was also very insistent about our knowing at every moment what our characters wanted. He often said, "Art is not like life. Art cannot be like life, because in life most people do not know what they want. But the actor must always know what the character wants. The character must always have clear-cut Objectives!" And Chekhov went even further. He said, "For the actor, it is not enough to simply have an Objective—nor even to feel a tepid desire for something. You must visualize the Objective as constantly being fulfilled. For example, if your Objective is 'I want to escape from this room,' then you must see yourself escaping, perhaps in many different ways—through the door, through the window, etc. It is the vision of the Objective being fulfilled that creates the impulse for a strong desire. This is what will bring your role to life."

Chekhov consistently encouraged me to discover the differences between the character's personality and my own. "It is the differences which the actor must portray, that is what makes the performance artistic and interesting," he said. "The similarities will be there by themselves!" Of course, in motion pictures and television, where typecasting is the rule rather than the exception, leading actors are often discouraged from using strong characterizations. Nevertheless, Chekhov believed that there is no sense in being an actor if one cannot transform oneself. I once heard him say, "Even if you think that the character is exactly like you, at least give her a crooked little finger!"

TAKING DIRECTION

The filming of one particular movie posed a great problem for me. The director and I did not see eye to eye on anything. We often disagreed even over the meaning of lines of dialogue. I was sure I was right. He was sure he was right. He had the time to take the scene again and again in order to achieve his interpretation. It was a particularly painful process for me because inwardly I fought him all the way—even when I was attempting to give him what he wanted. The result was, quite naturally, that my performance ended up being neither his way nor my way—only a kind of mishmash.

When the movie was completed I asked Chekhov to teach me how to take direction. Three fascinating sessions followed during which he gave me many difficult or seemingly impossible suggestions, for example, picking up an object and moving from the light into the darkness to look at it, or rushing into a room full of people to reveal to them a great discovery you have just made, yet turning your back to them to tell about it. When I would say, "Yes, but why—?" or "Yes, but how—?" Chekhov would say, "Don't think about it, don't talk about it—*do it!*" In other words, don't try to "figure it out," don't ask yourself, "Why would I [my character] do that?" Don't try to mentally justify it. Just *do it.* If necessary, do it more than one time. Suddenly there will come a moment when you feel, "Ah! Yes, that *is* possible. I see or experience it in a new way. I can make it work and I can do it artistically and truthfully!"

Exercising with "impossible suggestions," sooner or later you will discover that everything is psychologically justifiable. Even if at first a director's suggestion seems like insanity, your own creative, inner unconscious, without any help or interference from your intellect, has the power instantly to justify the action and make it possible for you to perform it truthfully.

Exercising to become convinced of this fact is particularly valuable for the film actor because many times he is asked to play a scene in a particular manner simply because the camera has already been set up in a certain way—even before the actors are blocked or rehearsed. At times the "setup" may require you to have your back to another character during a line that you feel should be spoken directly to the other character. A common cry of the Method actor is "I don't feel it that way." But unless you are already a big star, if you insist on *your* interpretation, you run the risk of either being replaced or never working for that director again. Enjoying your own flexibility gives you a marvelous tool for working in motion pictures and television.

CRITICISM IS A POISON

Working with Michael Chekhov both privately and in class was always both exhilarating and nourishing. You were always free to dare when you worked with Chekhov, for he both taught and lived his conviction that criticism is a poison, and that it is even more of a poison for the one who criticizes

than for the persons who are criticized. He taught that per-
ceiving what is wrong in any situation should only be a first
step in discovering a means for correcting the problem.

We were taught to rehearse or exercise only one aspect or
technique at a time. We might work only on Atmosphere or
only on the use of an Imaginary Body or only on using Objectives. We might rehearse this one aspect many times, until it
was really a solid and reliable part of our performance. Chekhov taught us never to allow our actor's critical judgment,
"our inner policeman," as he called it, to be at work while we
were actually performing. After each rehearsal or exercise,
however, Mischa would ask us to take a moment and silently
review what we had done. We were to ask ourselves, "To what
degree did I achieve what I set out to do? How strongly did
I create an Atmosphere? Did I truly experience this Imaginary
Body? Did the Objective I chose really impel me to action?"
and so forth. And if we had not been participating in the
exercise but had been only observing others, we were to ask
ourselves if we thought that the other actors had achieved
what they set out to do. If we felt that they did not achieve
it, he insisted that we put the question to ourselves "What
could they have done to make it better or stronger?"

After we had taken our silent review time, Chekhov would
say, "Good." Then he would proceed to tell us, "To my mind
you did achieve it," or "To my mind you did not achieve it.
You lost it at such and such a point," or "You lost your
concentration when you said. . . ." And Mischa always had
a suggestion for how to make it better.

ESPECIALLY FOR FILM

The following are techniques that were designed specifically
to help the actor who works before a camera.

"VEILING" FOR THE CAMERA

Chekhov believed in exploring the full scope, depth, and power of emotions, and in Radiating energy with the utmost strength. He encouraged us to let our emotions pour out fully, even explosively, in rehearsals (especially while preparing a part at home or in class). The camera, however, magnifies a hundredfold each facial expression and each flicker of an eye. In front of a camera the actor must be extremely economical in the use of gesture and facial expression. Unfortunately, this fact often encourages naturalistic, banal acting that contains no emotional depth. The actor has little "presence" on the screen and the performance is boring.

Actors often hear the admonition "Do less." Chekhov would have said "Do more, but 'veil' it." In other words, increase the strength of your Radiation, call up the emotions that you want until you are filled to the brim, and then imagine that a soft gossamer "veil" descends upon you, "veiling" your expression. If you try to "do less" you may kill the emotion. The image of the "veil," however, when invoked many times, in many different highly emotional moments, leads to great power. It results in both an economy of expression and real "presence," which the audience experiences. You may picture the "veil" as enveloping you totally or it may only be in front of your face. The veil can descend upon you from above or come from below. You can also endow the "veil" with color, a pale pink or a blue transparent "veil," according to your psychological need and the particular scene you are playing.

Chekhov taught a related technique that is especially helpful for reaction close-ups. Allow the emotion to build up within and "simmer," then simply listen to other characters and "think" an unbroken line of the character's thoughts while allowing the facial muscles to be as relaxed as possible.

A "LITTLE PIECE OF ART"

Though Chekhov loved being on the stage, he did not always enjoy working in front of a camera. By the time I met him, however, he had come to thoroughly enjoy film making. He told me that the discontinuity of action did not bother him at all; he had actually come to enjoy acting in "little pieces." He said, "Each small section has a beginning, a middle, and an end and should be thought of as a little piece of art." He often had me exercise small moments, bearing in mind that I was about to create "a little piece of art."

I would say to myself, "I begin," and pick up a glass; "Middle," drink the water; and set the glass down. "The End. That was a little piece of art!"

Michael Chekhov adapted to film by taking this attitude toward "small sections." Perhaps his love for what can be done with a small moment is best illustrated in a scene in *Spellbound* where, as the old professor, he lights his pipe, spilling the box of matches as he exclaims, "My doctor told me not to smoke but I am too nervous!" This moment is certainly "a little piece of art"—a beautiful, faceted jewel.

SHORTCUTS

A note of warning: The following "shortcuts" are not meant to replace the dedicated study of the detailed techniques or the systematic practice of the exercises in this book. The "shortcuts" alone are not calculated to develop each actor's unique creativity and in some cases might even reinforce "cliché acting" if used before the repeated practice of the exercises needed to put the actor in firm contact with his or her own "Center" and "Creative Individuality."

SHORTCUTS FOR PREPARATION AT HOME

Read the script silently as many times as possible.
Resist the temptation to say your lines aloud for as long as you can. Do not try to analyze or even consciously think about the script or the part. This allows your creative unconscious the greatest possible freedom in bringing forth a truly original interpretation of the role.

Describe the plot of the script to a friend.
The friend may be actually present or only imagined. Be sure to describe your character and the part your character plays in the story. Do not prepare this description ahead of time. It must be spontaneous. After you finish, take a moment to silently review what you have said. After a little practice you will be surprised how much unconscious wisdom and under-standing of the script and character you already possess.

"Baptize" the emotional sections.
This means to find successive sections in your script and name each one according to its principal emotion, feeling, or sensations, so that from the emotional point of view each section will differ from the next ones. For example, let us say that one section is "fear," another "doubt," and a third might be "courage." Having named these sections, which shouldn't be too small—the larger the better—begin reading your part in the "fear" section with the Quality or feeling that you found suitable for this particular section. Read it as many times as necessary until you feel that your lines become more and more expressive from the point of view of "fear." Then repeat the process with the sections you have baptized "doubt," "courage," and so on. Chekhov suggested that while reading your part in this manner you at first read only with your eyes, and then begin to whisper the lines incor-porating "fear," "doubt," "courage," etc., without allowing yourself to use your voice fully. Chekhov warned that if the

actor uses full voice prematurely, "All your fear of the part, of the lines, all your habits and the clichés that you would like to avoid, may awaken immediately and plunge into this loud voice of yours!"

The suggestion of working with and "baptizing emotional sections" may seem to some readers to encourage "result acting," i.e., deciding upon an appropriate emotion and then attempting to "play" it. However, after exercising this technique for a while (preferably with parts you are *not* going to play), you will find that the outcome is quite the opposite of "result acting." The emotions and feelings that are within every one of us are so rich, so boundless, that once we learn to trust ourselves and plunge into the world of emotion that is opened up by the words "fear," "doubt," "courage," "hate," "love," etc., we cause this sea of emotion and feeling to vibrate around us and within us. Soon you will get so many kinds of "fears," so many "doubts," "courages," and so on, that infinite nuances will "happen" for you.

You may also find that other "names" for sections that occur to you quite spontaneously have power to arouse your artistic interest or emotions. While working with "courage," for instance, an image might arise that would cause you to rename this section "lion tamer in a cage." Do not be afraid to allow your Creative Imagination to rebaptize sections.

Make a list of your character's physical activities.
Include those that are given in the script and those that you may wish to invent for this part. Then begin to fulfill the Activities, moving with different Qualities and in different Tempos that you sense will be suitable for these sections. It does not matter that you may never be able to use the business you invent once you reach the set. Once you have mastered this way of working, you will be able to adjust yourself to any director and to any circumstance. You will even be able to "rebaptize" the sections on the set to accommodate new

ideas that come to you as you begin to work with the director and other actors.

SHORTCUTS FOR PREPARATION ON THE SET

Make friends with the set.
You arrive on the set having never seen it before. You are really in an alien environment, but the script calls for your character to be comfortable there. There is no time for adequate rehearsal—perhaps for one quick run-through before the director calls, "Action!" Of course, if you are skillful you can fake being comfortable regardless of how nervous you may be, but it is extremely doubtful that you will be satisfied with your performance in the scene. Is there anything that can help? Yes. Chekhov gave the following suggestion. As early as possible before the rehearsal—perhaps while the crew is lighting—really make friends with everything on the set. You can envision stepping into the set as a kind of "crossing of a threshold" into a friendly realm. Touch the table, sit in the chair. You get something quite different when you touch a metal chair than when you touch a wooden chair. As soon as you make a mental note of an object's particular sensation or texture, you are friends with it. You may not be called upon actually to sit in that chair during the forthcoming scene, but acquaint yourself with it anyway! Make friends with the entire set. Endow the furniture with a kind of life through the use of your imagination. When you do, all those inanimate objects become your allies. Soon you begin to get something from them, invisibly as well as from the physical feel of them. You learn to develop through your own forces immediate relationships with what otherwise remain merely inanimate objects, and this adds greatly to your comfort. As with all techniques, it takes practice to learn to apply it quickly. When you first try for full awareness of the set, it may require more time than you have. Even a little effort and

awareness helps, however. At the very least, really *look* at the set—even from the sidelines—and silently say to as many objects as possible, "I greet you, I greet you."

Make friends with the camera.
All actors need to feel appreciated. They also need reassurance. Often the actors who project an aura of abrasive confidence are precisely the ones who most need reassurance and approval. Chekhov said that "reassuring the actor" was one of the principal functions of the director. Unfortunately, many directors—especially in television—either have not discovered this obvious truth or are too harried by the "TV time crunch" to put a priority on imparting confidence to the actor. How then does the actor satisfy this fundamental need to be appreciated? Chekhov suggested that the actor should "make friends" with the camera. Silently "greet" it at the beginning of each day you work before it. With your all-powerful Imagination, endow the camera with a friendly personality that appreciates and delights in every nuance you bring to the role you are playing. This is also an invaluable technique for actors who tend to "hide" from the eye of the camera. Some actors are really quite free and creative in rehearsals but contract noticeably once the camera begins to roll. You will not "hide" from a camera that you have made into a friend. You will Radiate to it more fully and confidently, and, as Chekhov would say, "Who knows? Perhaps an uncomfortable moment will suddenly, magically, become comfortable, even inspired."

Make friends with the audience.
Chekhov believed that it was important for actors to be aware of how much they really need and love their audiences. He said that when actors are not conscious of this love, or are ashamed of it, they are in danger of becoming jaded and patronizing toward the audience. These attitudes are especially prevalent in regard to television audiences, whom the

actor never sees. Chekhov suggested that both television and motion picture actors make a practice of visualizing their audiences—sitting at home or in theatres and imagining the audience as being interested in, learning from, and *enjoying* every nuance of the actor's performance.

Chekhov advised that while working in front of a camera, you create an "instant audience" by inwardly "greeting" the cameraperson and camera crew, gradually widening your awareness to include all the crew. Crew members are your live audience and certainly the audience that is most immediately accessible to you. Consciously establishing an inner relationship with them brings something more human into mechanized media. "Greeting the crew" does not mean shaking hands and getting to know each of them personally, although whenever possible, that, too, may be valuable for both actor and crew member. This "contact," as Chekhov means it, is really an invisible but conscious deed on the part of the actor. It is a Radiating of goodwill to the crew while sending them the thought, "I am performing for you and you are a wonderful audience who is there supporting me."

LOOKING TOWARD A FUTURE THEATRE

During the last years of Chekhov's work, he frequently called upon each of us as actors to develop clear concepts and visualizations of what we believe an *Ideal Theatre** should be for the future. He himself envisioned a theatre that, among many other things, does not confuse "naturalism" with "realism" and that can entertain the public with diverse theatrical styles. Chekhov's vision of a future theatre also called for a sense of moral responsibility on the part of producers, direc-

*In the context of Ideal Theatre, the word "theatre" includes stage, motion pictures, television, and any medium in which the actor is called upon to perform.

tors, and writers, as well as actors. He said they must be willing to ask, "What effect will our production have upon the audience? What will be stirred up within the spectators? Will what we are presenting have any positive value for them as human beings?" Chekhov wanted those who develop productions to ask themselves if the members of their audience will be strengthened in some way by what they have seen—or will they actually become weaker through their encounter with the play or screenplay.

Those who have worked seriously with Michael Chekhov's Technique know that each aspect, when exercised sufficiently, becomes a gift to the actor, not only as an artist but also as a human being—a gift that can become nourishment for the human spirit, given through the actor to the world.

INDEX

MALA POWERS, who wrote the Preface and Afterword for this book, has starred on Broadway, television, radio, and in more than twenty-six motion pictures, including her critically acclaimed portrayal of Roxane opposite José Ferrer in *Cyrano de Bergerac*. In addition, she enjoys a successful writing career in the United States, Great Britain, and elsewhere in Europe, where her books *Follow the Year* (HarperSanFrancisco) and *Follow the Star* have been translated into several languages.

As an aspiring young actress, Mala met Michael Chekhov in California and studied with him extensively, both privately and in classes during the last six years of his life. She was accepted into his home and embraced by both him and his wife, Xenia, almost as a daughter. Before Xenia Chekhov's death in 1970, she named Mala executrix of the Chekhov Estate. In recent years, in addition to writing and acting, Mala has been teaching the Chekhov Technique. Currently, she is preparing an audiocassette collection of Michael Chekhov's actual recorded talks on "Theatre and the Art of Acting," to be published by Applause Books, making them available to the public for the first time.

MEL GORDON is Professor of Dramatic Art at the University of California, Berkeley. A former teacher at the Michael Chekhov Studio in New York, he is the author of seven books on acting and theatre. His most recent book, *The Grand Guignol*, was nominated for the Bernard Hewitt Award for Best Book on the Performing Arts.